i

Have a Plan and Plan to Act

Have a Plan and Plan to Act

A Guide for Successful,

Victorious Living

in

Tumultuous Times

Book 1

By

Phoenix Rising

Published 2012

Printed in the United States of America

ISBN 978-1470011116

Second Edition - collector series.

The journey of life takes us many places and down many roads and while on this journey we encounter many souls.

Sometimes we are so very blessed to find a soul that is so tender and so loving that we make the choice to no longer walk alone but to walk this journey hand in hand with this kind and loving soul we have found. It is so with my beloved wife L.H. I have learned many things during my life along this journey and one of the greatest lessons learned is that everything happens for a reason....everything.

Have a plan and plan to act.

Phoenix

CONTENTS

INTRODUCTION

Introduction

I've been heard to say many times for people to have a plan and plan to act.

But just what exactly do I mean when I say this?

Well to be clear I mean exactly what I say... we should as responsible human beings during these tumultuous times we live in have a plan in place for ourselves and our loved ones that we may be able to deal with any situation that may come our way.

I know that it is impossible to prepare for everything but I do know it is possible to prepare for many of the things that could come into our lives in such a way to disrupt our normal way of living.

To live a successful and victorious life requires joy, peace and focus. But to have the joy, peace and focus required to live a successful, victorious life we must be free from both stress and fear.

But how does one live free from stress and fear while being surrounded by the woes of these tumultuous times? We see the world on the brink of warfare...we see the global economy failing...we see this separation between the "haves" and "have not's" ever widening on a daily basis.

Everywhere we turn there seems to be messages of warning and trouble ahead.

The news headlines and the news media are constantly pumping fear and uncertainty into the psyche of the masses. I feel that this constant onslaught of fear, doom and negativity is allowed and controlled by design. But you ask...why would this be so? I believe the reason for this constant onslaught of negative information that seems to flood the airwaves around us bringing this undue stress to the public could be twofold. One reason is for control and the other reason is for monetary gain by those who pour forth the images of fear, doubt and uncertainty which results in undue stress on the public plus adding constant uncertainty, doubts and fear in the minds of the public resulting in fearful masses seeking answers and direction...both of which the media masters and those behind the scenes are more than willing to provide. This is how "the few" control "the many"

In this book I address the current situation we face on Earth as well as present practical solutions and guidelines that will aid the reader to rise from the ashes of fear and uncertainty of this world, to take wing rising above any situation we may face to soar high into the clean, clear skies, to a joyful life of successful, victorious living.

Now is the time to wake up...

Now is the time to say no to fear...

Now is the time to rise above!

1

Welcome to Life

So here you are...

At the writing of this book we are in the beginning of the year 2012...the infamous, ominous year of...2012.

(Insert dramatic music here)

Leading up to this year we have seen much anticipation and much speculation. We have all of the talk and writing of the Mayan calendar prophesies plus movies of doom to boot as well we have the ever deteriorating global economic and geopolitical situation.

The uncertainty of what may happen in this era is having a visible and recordable effect upon all society.

Things have changed quickly on earth and the changes we have witnessed within society and the decline of moral standards over the past few decades is nothing less than remarkable.

This amazing and shocking decline of moral and ethical behavior is, I feel, a direct result of the constant onslaught of distraction and entertainment we find ourselves surrounded with on a 24hr. basis.

It is as if all of humanity has been surrounded by a constant din of unending electronic noise.

Television, the Internet, the radio, music players, cell phones and every other form of distraction the marketers can conceive and let us not forget gaming.

It is this constant distraction of entertainment that prevents us as human beings from conducting personal meditative introspection. It is this lack of personal introspection that has led to the drastic decline of moral standing in modern society.

So how did it get like this? What brought us to this point where people are so overcome with a constant distraction and stress that they have no time to think?

I feel the true reason behind this current situation is nothing less than greed and the lust for power of those who would seek to control and exploit all of mankind for personal gain. We're looking at a situation that has been created by design with great care and for two very specific reasons. The first and foremost reason is greed.

The greed and desire to manipulate the minds of the masses into buying products they do not need so the corporate profits will increase. We see a constant onslaught of electronic mind manipulation from the ad agencies like a nonstop assault upon the senses.

The televisions blast a non-stop message of "Buy this and buy that! If you own this item you will be happy! If you look like this airbrushed model everyone will like you! Smart people own this expensive item and sexy people buy these expensive clothes!"

This is nothing less than electronic mind control pure and simple, driven deep into the psyche of unknowing victims by visually and audibly implanting electronic overlay. Exciting visual and audible overlays laced with overt sexuality which result in the chemical stimulation of the brain's most base centers of desire. This is all done while the viewer has been induced into nothing less than a trance like mental state.

Has it always been this way?

No it has not. There was a time many decades ago when products were advertised and offered for their value. And in those times people purchased products based upon their value, strength and durability. Of course the beauty of the product along with its functionality has always been held in high esteem and examples of this are seen throughout all of history. In fact one of the trademarks of true craftsmanship and value has been the flowing combination of beauty and functionality along with strength and durability.

But this all changed and changed for a reason.

Allow me to give as an example a product such as a simple biscuit mix. Many decades ago a good biscuit mix would have been advertised for how fine of a product it was and the quality of the biscuits it produced. But something changed and that change came when advertisers realized that they could lure more customers into buying their products if in addition to highlighting the quality of their product they also implanted the message that if a customer where to buy and use their product they would become a happier person. Now this lure of promised happiness with the purchase of the advertised product was not based upon the value, functionality or durability of the product advertised but instead the advertisers began to inject the impression and idea into the minds of the public that the use or ownership of their product could do miraculous things for the buyer.

What type of miraculous things? For the most part the advertisements promised love, adoration, success, beauty and

3

th! Gone were the days when a biscuit mix was touted ... flavor and value but instead it the call went forth that if you use that biscuit mix he would "love you forever" or some other false promise made by the advertisers having nothing to do with the value of the product but everything to do with tricking the public into buying overpriced items they did not need. So began the science of manipulating the minds of the masses for monetary gain.

Now when all of this began in printed media it was one thing but soon this type of advertising moved from print to radio to television and now during this time it is also deeply imbedded in music and movies and has had such an impact and I would say, negative impact, on society it has stolen the very sanctity of personal solitude and peace of mind, from most persons, both young and old in modern society. Subduing free and critical thought form with mass induced hypnotic suggestion all for the control and gain of those controlling the media and advertising.

I've spoken in the past about "Plato's Allegory of the Cave". In this parable of the cave which the Greek philosopher Plato wrote in his work "The Republic" Plato allows Socrates to describe a group of people who have lived inside a cave all of their lives as prisoners chained to the wall only being able to see the blank wall before them. Behind the prisoners is an enormous fire and in between the fire and the prisoners is a raised walkway and along this walkway the very people who control the prisoners carry large objects in front of the light of the fire which in turn cast huge frightful images on the cave wall in front of the prisoners. These large and frightful images along with frightful sounds, give the false illusion to the prisoners that they are being over watched and controlled by great and powerful beings.

These false images and the fear it creates is how the "few prison keepers" control the "many prisoners".

If the prisoners were free to turn their heads and see the truth of the situation, seeing that the controllers are not great and mighty beings but are only men and women just like themselves, who have tricked them by the use of the false flickering images on the cave wall. The prisoners could be free of the illusion and then free from the fear...the very fear that controls all aspects of their lives if they only knew the truth. So how is it that something written by Plato around 380 BC is relevant to today's situation?

Many of the listeners to my radio program "Phoenix Rising Radio" have heard me reference in the past the Plato's allegory of the cave but I have changed the name slightly reflecting todays modern situation to the "Man Cave Wall". And in this "Man Cave" of the modern home the blank wall has been replaced with the flat screen TV. Not much else has changed as we have those who control the masses still doing so by casting frightful images on the "man cave" wall. Images of war....images of violence...images of economic chaos. All of which instill fear, doubt, stress and uncertainty upon the masses. It is this very fear that is being used as a tool of control, inducing stress and it is this stress that makes people fearful and ill. Our society is plagued with so called stress disorders. Anxiety medications are given out like candy but this candy is not free. The pharmaceutical giants make billions in profits from the distribution of these so called anti-anxiety drugs. Not only are the pharmaceutical giants the financial winners in this game but so are the doctors, hospitals, clinics and pharmacies. The profits are astronomical!

So fear and the active distribution of fear is big business! It has been said that one in five adults in the United States are currently on one of these pre-scribed anti-anxiety medications. I'm sure some of the readers of this book are also users of these prescribed medications as the numbers and statistics would support that assumption.

Now, the results of the free flowing distribution of anti-anxiety medications are more than massive corporate profits but also have the added intentional effect of the chemical mind altering power to induce even deeper hypnotic states within the minds of masses and by doing so increase the power of suggestion and control that the media has upon the minds of those whom are drugged.

So, the very flickering images on the man cave wall that induce this fear that causes the anxiety that in turn causes the viewer to seek out help from their health professional (as advised by the commercials) have effectively created a large base of viewers in the world who have unwillingly submitted themselves to being influenced by these images into becoming nothing less than the perfect mind control subject.

So, here we have millions of people in the world under the influence of mind altering substances, some prescribed some self-induced subjecting themselves to a constant onslaught of electronic images assaulting their minds and driving them deeper into heightened emotional states of fear, greed, lust, anger and uncertainty. This is all been done for two reasons and those two reasons are greed and power.

Life changed so much in so many ways with the advent of scientific advances in technology. Intelligence and self-awareness has grown by leaps and bounds and this is a good thing. But we also see that those who would control the masses for greed and power are exerting pressure and suppression of many technologies that could change the world.

We have all heard the stories of groundbreaking technologies, phenomenal discoveries made by the inventors who had made incredible discoveries and who have created incredible devices that could be inexpensively reproduced that would change the world forever.

Water powered engines, hydrogen generators, advanced solar devices and many more amazing devices and discoveries all of which could change the world in which we live. So where are these devices? So where are these inventions?

They are being suppressed and hidden and they are being suppressed to prevent the loss of profits from large energy companies. This suppression borders on criminal behavior and is without a doubt immoral.

The life that we live at the time of this writing is one of great control and suppression of thought. The powers that be are intensifying their efforts at this time to stop a great awakening. A great awakening of the sleeping masses, for not all have been tricked by the flickering images on the man cave wall, and many being awakened to the truth, that things are not as they seem, are beginning to ask the real questions and are beginning to demand real answers.

We saw this awakening beginning strongly in 2011 with the "Arab Spring" movements and the "Occupy" movements that erupted worldwide. Many people claimed that the Occupy Wall Street movement was nothing more than a political stunt paid for and orchestrated by those in control. The exact true origins of this movement that sprang up globally may never be known but what is known is that the seed was planted into the hearts and minds of the masses and now as this seed begins to bloom the people are calling out for change.

While observing this phenomenon one of the first things I noticed was that the media masters, they who control the masses, were doing their best to not cover the situation which told me the event was indeed not staged by those who seek to control but was in fact a true wellspring of emotional uprising in the hearts of people.

A lot of the reality of the situation and some of the things that were said on the streets by the people were never reported in the press at all but were relayed and reported by the people's media which is nothing more than people recording live as it happened on cell phones and small camcorders being live streamed or later uploaded on the internet. Amazing speeches were given and some heart-breaking displays of emotional outpouring from those who feel as if there is little or no hope.

We are witnessing at this time the beginnings of the failure of the greed system, the very greed system and control system that drives it all. In an effort to milk as much money from the public as they can, the corporations and banks have pushed the people to the very breaking point.

They have created a system motivated by greed and lust whose driving force has pushed the limits to the extreme and the point at which the public will not be pushed any further has almost been reached...and when that point has been reached....look out.

History has shown that when an oppressed people are pushed beyond the breaking point, there are no walls high enough, nor doors strong enough to protect those who have abused their positions of power over the people, to exploit and steal from the masses inducing a backlash of violent rage and wrath they themselves, the controllers have created.

People in modern society have been tricked into thinking that if they did not own certain products, drive certain cars, visit certain places or shop at certain stores they would not be happy, they would not be successful, they would not be sexy and because of all of this they would not be loved if they did not use or buy the products offered.

This unrealistic stress placed upon the population by the media for the profit of the corporations is a curse upon mankind, breeding the stress which causes illness in modern society. But again as stated before this illness is big business, illness creates huge profits for the giant pharmaceutical corporations.

I heard an interesting resting word used the other night by someone while describing the current state of assault society is facing from giant pharmaceutical corporations, the word they used was "Pharmageddon" which of course a combination of the two words pharmaceutical and Armageddon thus "Pharmageddon". To this I will add.... The old school saying, "many a truth is said in jest."

But there is change afoot...people are beginning to break away from the media control and because of this we're seeing strong and swift reaction from the governments of the world. We are witnessing at this time some very draconian legislation that has been passed or is about to be passed and by the time this book goes to print may well indeed be history.

We're seeing an effort by the governments to control information like never before.

I have said many times knowledge is power and we are witnessing the great increase of knowledge by the Internet and the radio that is awakening the sleeping masses to the truth of the situation that they have been controlled and tricked.

They are tricked into behaving in such a way and into believing certain things that has cause them to blindly react to visual impulses implanted by the media through television, resulting in the transfer of their wealth, from their hard work into the bank accounts of the big banks and corporations while receiving in return, overpriced cheaply made objects that had subliminally promised by the media would bring them personal fulfillment, success, beauty and love.

The people have awakened to the fact that by falsely chasing these claims it has gotten them nowhere but into debt. Massive debt! The entire world is in debt! The corporations and the banks have created a situation using the tool of the media and their psychological mind control into tricking most of the population into a position of self-imposed servitude.

This is corporate slavery, plain and simple. The people now seeing this situation for what it is are beginning to speak out and not only speak out but to also take it to the street! The powers that be seeing that they are beginning to lose control of the situation are tightening their grip even more. I have compared this situation to a fruit tree. It is said that fruit trees right before they die will fruit the heaviest.

We are now witnessing the heavy fruiting of the tree of tyrannical government control. We see proposed legislation to limit free speech not only on the Internet but also free speech and gatherings in public in an effort to prevent even more of the public from hearing the truth and that truth being, things are not as they seem.

One of the unfortunate results that we have witnessed because of this rampant corporate greed is the destabilization of the entire global economic system. And this situation is very dangerous. Historically when governments get into a condition of dire economic duress with no logical solution, we see drastic economic changes within the economy of that nation that always seem to have an extremely negative affect up-on the population while still benefiting those in power.

This is commonly the result of the devaluation of the nation's currency or the actual seizure of the assets and wealth of the populace. We have seen historical examples of this all over the world including in the last century the United States.

Unfortunately the other result we see when we witness nations in serious economic duress is warfare.

There is a cycle that has been witnessed throughout history, one of war, boom and then economic bust. Many nations immediately after warfare if they have been victorious, experience robust economic growth. This comes from the basic mechanics of warfare. You have a large part of the working population shifted to the military thus opening up all type of jobs. Next we see a surge in manufacturing to support the war machine churning out all types of products and machinery designed to kill.

We see massive contracts and high paying jobs offered to the adventurous willing to place themselves in harm's way. We see many wounded and hospitalized which increases the profits of the pharmaceutical giants.

We see increased news coverage pandering to the fears of the public who are desperate to find in the news any word of what may be truly be going on. All of this of course increases stress and this increase of stress will cause the populace to seek escape through fantasy and entertainment and because of this desire to escape the reality and horrors of warfare the profits of the entertainment industry soar as do the profits of the drug and alcohol companies.

So, during the war cycle, because of increased demand and increased job availability, the base manufacturing economy surges, as does the entertainment and distraction economy.

What I define as the distraction economy would be the elements and products used by those who would control, to distract the populace from the reality at hand.

Now I will admit much of this distraction is actively sought out by most and some on a healthy basis, as it should be by those who live balanced and healthy lives, but done so by thoughtful selection, based upon value and moderation.

This war cycle if not well controlled can have an adverse effect on a nation's economy as we have seen many times throughout history by the basic precept that the spoils of war are to the victor.

I would like to add, that during warfare, lives lost for the economic gain of others are lives that are lost in vain....and that is the true tragedy of warfare, and in that regard there are no true victors in any warfare.

Next, after the active cycle of warfare a nation will witness the return of its troops, a revitalization of the nation's psyche, and the continued surge of the economy. Depending upon different factors the length of this economic revitalization and the depths of same will vary but is becoming very apparent that these post war economic up-swings are having much less or no effect at all.

After the traditional economic revitalization post warfare, we will see the system worn down through the greed.

At this point because of the excessive usury of the banks and corporations all profits brought into the coffers by the warfare have been bled dry thus leading to the final part of the cycle, which is economic failure. This post war economic failure is where we see the world at right now. We are witnessing in this war, boom and bust cycle a compression of same to the point that the linear time be-tween the cycle of prosperity and economic collapse is ever becoming less and less. The obvious conclusion that most rational minds would make is that this continued behavior of killing for profit is destined for failure. But what we are witnessing at the time of this writing in the early part of 2012 is the fast build up to nothing less than world war three. Nations all across the globe are in economic duress. The G20, the IMF, the U.N. and all other global organizations are seeking solutions but in all of this we have a serious problem and that serious problem is that those who would control the masses for profit are the very ones in control of the world and in control of all key positions of power.

This means for them to discontinue the war for profit cycle that has led to their massive wealth at the demise of all others must go on at all cost. If not, they that control would lose that which they hold most precious, that being the total control of the minds and wealth of others through fear and emotional manipulation.

So welcome to the world!

Here we are, the year 2012 teetering on the precipice of Armageddon, living in a world totally under control of greedy individuals whose only desire is to take the wealth of others, control the thoughts, minds, desires and actions of all below them with no regard of the outcome as long as their comfort level remains high. They in power feel they can continue with their plans of initiating their next phase of wealth generation which would be World War Three also known as...Armageddon.

At this Point I would like to say one of the primary reasons for this book is to aid the reader in gaining clarity of purpose and intent.

Because of the media induced stupor that has enveloped the minds of most from birth, with constant distraction an onslaught of fear, excitement and mental stimulation, people have been robbed!

People have been robbed of not only their wealth but also of their ability to think clearly.

This fact that people can no longer take time to think and contemplate their own thoughts and actions has actually placed the populace into harm's way.

How is this you ask?

The reason I say this is because the constant rush of life that people are caught in constantly trying to make ends meet and constantly trying to achieve the false desires placed into their minds and hearts by the media, has removed the ability of logical thought and reasoning, which in former days was the very foundation of a well prepared and moral society.

We have touched upon the moral issues or lack thereof if you will, which comes from the lack of proper self-introspection of our actions and deeds.

But what this book addresses is one of the other resulting dysfunctional aspects that the population suffers from because of this overt corporate driven media mind control, and that is, the lack of proper planning.

People suffer from such an onslaught of nonstop media manipulation that the very basic human trait, exhibited by our ancestors throughout history of being prepared for potential basic needs in our lives in the event of shortages, supply disruptions, or disasters both natural and man-made, is all but gone. This trait once common in all peoples is all but lost in today's world. If we stop and turn off the TV, lay down the distractions and take the time to objectively and honestly look at our true situations we face in the world at this time, we will see the potential for disruptions and shortages and then realize the pressing need to have a serious plan in place. One might ask why is it that the powers that be would not want the population to be prepared in the event of disaster?

Do they want the masses so distracted that they could not care for themselves? The answer to that question is YES! They want that very thing, but only to the extent that would allow their transition into a position of more control without exasperating and enraging the population into action against those in control. This is why we see the ads telling people to visit FEMA web sites for preparedness suggestions. These are good guidelines as a start but they only touch upon one part of the equation that being physical preparation which is very important, but what we will cover in this book is a plan of action for total preparation of the heart, mind, soul and body.

And to do this we must honestly without distraction assess our situation...saying no to fear. I say this often "say no to fear". What am I saying when I say this? When I say no to fear I am saying no to doubt, uncertainty and threat. We all understand the fear constantly pushed by the media.

It is because of this fear that we have doubt. This fear makes us doubt our own safety, our own security and our own future. One of the major tools the media and the powers that be have used to instill fear in the population is the lie that you are all alone. We must keep things in perspective to the true situation in the world today, and that is that the entire world is on the brink of economic collapse! Banks and governments, who oppress the poor through excessive taxation and exorbitant high interest loans, put forward the lie that it is not their excessive greed and their deceptive practices that have caused the problem, but instead they blame the consumers and citizens themselves for the problems! They have put forward the lie that not only is it your fault, but they also attempt through careful manipulation to deceive the masses into thinking that they are alone in their problems. They put forward the message that it is not their excessive taxation and excessive and exorbitant banking fees that have created the problem, but that it is your personal irresponsibility that is the problem.

This is no different than if an adult were to hand to a child fine China plates and continued to do so until the amount was too heavy for the child to hold...resulting in the plates slipping from the child's hands crashing to the floor. Whose fault would be that the plates were broken? The child who was given more than he could handle? Or the adult who continued to overload the child knowing full well it was more than a child could handle? This is the exact situation we see today economically in the world.

We have seen the population intentionally overloaded with debt and taxation with the governments and banking institutions knowing full well it was more than could be carried by the consumer. And now that the economic situation has crashed to the floor the governments and banking institutions of the world wrongfully placed the blame upon the consumers.

We now see this active effort to shame those who have stumbled under this excessive load of debt and taxation and interest.

There is an attempt by the media to shame people into thining not only are they at fault but that they are also alone or in the minority.

This is done as a tool of control to instill fear and shame. This fear and shame add to the stress which fuels this state of "Pharmageddon." To say "NO" to all of this requires conscious action. And this conscious action can only come from a conscious attitude. We have heard philosophers and teachers of the past expound upon the wisdom of active consciousness or what some would call the act of "being here now". To take the proactive stance of "being here now" to consciously address the situation, we must first remove doubt, fear and distraction.

And to begin this process we must first begin by assessing the situation.

Before we begin the next section I would like to say that the whole reason for this work is to share with others the methods and ways I myself have learned in my life, to plan and organize any task, in such a way as to make the plan easy to follow and implement. Now as we know in life we see change all of the time and that very nature of change I have covered in the section on "contingency planning". Life is indeed a "live and fluid situation" and being able to bend and not break is vital for survival and growth.

We all want the same things in life and those basic desires are to not worry about having our needs met and being free from fear. One of the things I say all of the time is to "say no to fear". I say this because it is so important. It is doubt and fear that prevent clear thought. A great truth taught by many great spiritual teachers is that our mind and the thoughts we allow, are the very fuel that fires the engine of creation. "Thoughts become things" and what so ever you allow your mind to dwell upon, be it good or bad, results in the manifestation of your external reality. Now we must remember that we are not alone in this ability and that is why we see so much strife and turmoil on Earth. It is because of the constant manifestation of the minds of the masses that for the most part, dwell in constant fear, doubt and anger that we see such turmoil made manifest on Earth. So how do we deal with this situation?

What we must do is stay positive, always hoping for the best and doing our best to project the largest area of positive energy around us at all times. This way as the masses create negative realities and outcomes for themselves, our positive energies can counter their negative. This is why we need to prepare and have a plan, that we may have peace and plenty, in a world projecting lack and strife. Planning is not being fearful. Planning is being proactive and positive by saying NO to the fears projected all around.

Having a positive attitude is not always easy, the troubles we have in life, the sorrows we have in life, are all too often, all too frequent. And this is all part of the learning process. Even great teachers of the past who have come to our existence to teach us higher ways have stumbled with doubt. The reason for this is because it is part of the human existence...it is part of the human experience. It is through stress, strain and exertion that we gain strength. Just as the physical exercise, strain and exertion put forth better our very physical being. So in the same way that we strengthen our body through exertion and stress we can strengthen our minds and our souls through hardship. Everything...even the hard things are a blessing.

In the same manner that too much physical exertion is not beneficial, and tears down the body instead of it building it up, too much stress, too much grief and too much sorrow if not handled well can also break down the psyche. This is what happens during a nervous breakdown. People become so overburdened with the stress and sorrows of the world that they feel helpless and so over-burdened they just give up. People who get into this situation sometimes feel so helpless and so overcome with grief they even take their own lives.

The stress that we have seen placed upon this world by the hands of those who would control, is done so by greed. This greed to own it all, both power and wealth has perpetrated throughout time this great injustice and sorrow upon the people of the world. This injustice must stop NOW!

How much is enough? How much power can they hold? Where does it all stop? These questions are being asked by the people all over the world at this time and people are beginning to demand answers. These demands are being seen in the streets at this time. We have seen violent outbreaks in different parts of the world throughout the year 2011 and it is being projected that the year 2012 will be a time of public uprising.

I have said before, that when the people are pushed to the very limit that they can stand, when the people are pushed to economic breaking point, that point...is the point of violent backlash. We saw instances in 2011 where the people in power, the corporations and those in government positions, actually mocked and made fun of the people who had taken to the streets, trying to belittle them and to make them feel powerless. History shows that when we have a situation arise where people feel hopeless and overburdened by poverty and debt and are also being ruled over by wealthy elite who mock also them in their sorrow, the outcome of the situation is one of violence.

In that situation no walls are high enough; no door is strong enough...to keep the scorn of the masses from unleashing upon those who mock. And such is the situation the world is facing today. This social and geopolitical uncertainty is nothing less than a ticking time bomb and now is the time to consider these things and now is the time to make plans for your own protection and provision. Add to this the stress of geopolitical saber rattling, and the high potential of global warfare. The Middle East and situation is nothing less than the prelude to Armageddon and this situation will affect the entire world.

The fragility of our infrastructure and fragility of our supply chain is amazing. This weakness and frailty is the direct result of greed of the corporations. Always doing everything they can to cut corners and to make things as cheaply as possible. This cost cutting for profit became so rampant in the last part of the 20th century resulting in the deaths of many consumers, that a new agency had to be developed within the United States to deal with this greed based situation. It was the result of the grassroots uprising by the people who were harmed demanding something be done for their own protection. The car manufacturers and other industrial manufactures were producing products so poorly made and so cheaply made it was resulting in the death of many consumers.

This was no surprise to see as the corporations will push the limit with everything including death, for profit and until there it is a massive public outcry nothing is done. This sad fact is that many times those who have been injured by this rampant greed of the corporations are bought off to be silent. The big corporations know that money talks and the big corporations are all too willing to pay someone off just to make them go away. We face this very situation today with our electrical infrastructure. There has been a massive outcry by groups who have worked for years trying to lobby the United States government to place regulation upon the electrical industry that they would harden the infrastructure against EMP (electro-magnetic pulse). EMP can be naturally induced by solar storms or the result of weapons designed for that very purpose. But the corporations refuse and change because of the amount of money it would cost. So something must be done by YOU for your own protection.

2

Accessing the Situation

Step one: Turn off the television.

Step two: Stop fretting over the past.

Step three: Stop worrying about the future.

Step four: Be honest with your-self.

Step five: grab a pen a paper.

Welcome to right now.

When exactly is right now for you?

It could be near the time of the writing of this book in early 2012...before world war three. It could be some time in the middle of world war three...or it could be some time in the distant future. Whenever the time, it matters not, for two things hold true, one being that whenever it may be that you're reading this, it is "now" for you, and the other is, common sense does not have an expiration date.

What is your current situation?

You could be reading this on an e-reader in the comfort of a luxury home with ample bank accounts. Or you could be in a humble home or an apartment struggling to make ends meet. You could be in an urban environment, a suburban environment or in the middle of the wilderness. No matter where you are and no matter what your situation, be it one of wealth or one of lack, your situation can change in a moment's time. Also your current position, be it pre-war, during war or post warfare, does not matter in the need for you to personally assess your situation and the potential changes you may face in your lifestyle. The fact is, those living in luxury and comfort as they read this may be at the greatest disadvantage, as compared to those struggling to make ends meet at this current time in duress. How can this be you ask?

The reason I say this is that many who live in comfort, feeling they have all of their needs met, have been lulled into a false state of security. This false state of security has been perpetrated and reinforced by the media. There is a great deception among the people that if you have sufficient funding and luxurious surroundings then you are safe. I have found during my interesting life that many persons of wealth have fallen into this trap of false security. This false sense of security is based upon the misconception that our current form of electronic banking and paper based wealth system will continue on forever. This false sense of security of trusting our fragile infrastructure to always be there no matter what is not only foolhardy but potentially very dangerous. Most think if there are problems or disruptions with our electrical grid and the financial system that it supports, that those disruptions could be and would be quickly resolved, resulting in nothing more than a temporary inconvenience. While in most cases this is true there are situations that we are potentially facing on Earth that could create not just a temporary disruption but one that could last for many weeks or months and some even say there is the potential in fact of years of disruption! Now, that alone is a frightening thought if you allow yourself to fully contemplate the ramifications of such a situation. Those who now live a life of luxury are doing so with little to no regard of the very real possibility of losing all they have in a moment's notice. Now on the other hand those who find themselves at this time to be in need and perhaps struggling to make ends meet are in fact I feel, blessed to have been placed into this situation, where they must think about possible shortcomings in the future and how they must deal with this. But even so, most of these individuals are overcome by fear and doubt, allowing themselves at times to not think clearly while carefully making plans but instead only expressing worry and fret about what pains the future may hold and in doing so their stress levels become very high. I would like to say at this time that for people to be in a state of worry is nothing more than reveling in the state of fear itself and that is not only NOT a good thing but also it is potentially dangerous in more ways than one! So as we begin to assess the situation we must do so with a state of balance. This balance is very important to our proper planning as we assess our current situation making note of possible outcomes that could have a negative effect upon our lives. I always say that we must say NO to fear and this is paramount that we must learn to do so, for it is fear itself that prevents us from succeeding. When I speak of succeeding I mean the success needed to effectively and efficiently live our lives in a joyous and victorious way. For if we're seized with fear we will not *act*, we instead will *react*, and it is this reaction to fear that all too often is done in terror and haste which leads to disaster in our lives. When I say disaster one tends to think of a large disaster with everything falling apart and much damaged. What I mean when I speak of disasters I include even the little disasters that we can bring upon ourselves day to day by simply making the wrong decisions or by saying the wrong thing at the wrong time. So to begin successful, honest assessment of our situation we must begin by overcoming fear. Sometimes fear will prevent us from honestly seeking out the true facts. How many times have you seen this in your own life? Have you ever attempted to warn someone of something for their own good and they do not want to hear it? Or have you yourself experienced this? I know I have! It is part of growth. So it is important that we honestly look at our situation and honestly look at the unfolding present economic, social, political and environmental challenges we face at this time or that we may face in the very near future. The guidelines being put forth with in this book are the very basics which work for most situations you may find yourself in at this time, whenever that time may be. Again I would like to say that common sense and practical planning are timeless and no matter what your situation or standing, to "have a plan to and to plan act", is to have the stance of the responsible human being. By having a plan and acting upon your plan you'll find yourself to be less stressed and therefore healthier and more joyful and that is the key to a victorious life style. So just how do you assess your situation? Allow me to share with you some of what I have learned as part of my military training. As part of my long military training that lead up to and continued throughout my assignments in military special operations one of the first and primary skills you are taught is that of threat assessment. This is a skill that was once common among all human beings. We all do this in our own way to varying degrees on a daily basis. We notice things that could be dangerous, we veer out of the way of potholes in the road as we drive, we sometimes take note of someone who may appear suspicious...and even in small ways we exercise caution like tossing things from the refrigerator just to be on the safe side. It's human nature to watch out for danger but these simple safeguards are nothing less than the routine of the mundane. What we are addressing and assessing here are not the mundane and common dangers of the day but instead we must truthfully and honestly assess the social, political, economic and environmental dangers that have the potential to disrupt and alter our daily life styles on a moment's notice... with little to no warning. To begin your personal assessment of your current situation you must first rid yourself of distraction. Create for yourself some peace and quiet time, and if your situation allows also some solitude. Grab something to write with and a notepad to take notes or make a list. Once you have done this you may begin. Start off by making notes of the major global threats that are ongoing at this time that have the potential of affecting your personal lifestyle. Are there rumblings of warfare? If so how can this affect you in your location? Can this affect the economic situation that you are in? Does this potential warfare pose a threat to fuel supplies? If so how would this directly alter your life? One thing that many do not fully understand is that the potential disruption of fuel supplies to the west and most of Europe would directly result in food prices soaring. One of the latest estimates concerning the potential closing of the Straits of Hormuz is that the price for a barrel of oil could reach as high as $400 or more and this would translate into $8.00 a gallon gasoline at the pumps in the United States! The adverse effect this would have on the economy would be nothing less than devastating! This is just is just one possibility and this possibility could lead to food shortages as well as fuel shortages, limiting travel and possibly making some food items hard to get if not impossible to get. So that is one thing to consider ever present and threatening in this world at this time. At the time of this reading you may find yourself in this very situation.

If that is the case....that is OK and that is part of "assessing your situation". Also for many readers particularly those living in Europe major disruptions in the fuel supply could also affect and limit the ability to heat homes in the wintertime and that is something to consider. I will not go into detail in this book about the threats now facing our world as that is your personal responsibility, for as times and situations change those very threats will also change and the potential or probability of occurrence of these threats will change with time. To put it bluntly the situation dictates and only YOU can accurately assess YOUR current situation and any threats YOU may face. So what is *your* current situation? What are *your* current needs? What do you see as your most immediate threat or danger? When doing a threat assessment we need to begin from our very center location and work our way out. The reason for this is that the most dangerous threat to you could well be the closest one. When I say close I mean both close in proximity and time. Also, as you began your threat assessment, (which I do in circular form, by assessing the situation near me all around in 360° concentric circles) you must start with yourself! The first question you must honestly ask yourself is...are *you* a threat to *you*? Some may laugh when they read this, but some may not, for the sad truth is that sometimes people are their own worst enemies! To live a joyous and victorious life style is to live a life free from illness and pain. Sometimes in life afflictions will come, but sometimes we afflict *ourselves* with poor health and lack of energy by not caring for ourselves properly.

You know and I do not need to tell you that you should take care of yourself.

You know the right things to eat and how much too eat as well as what habits you may have that are not healthy. This book is about personal responsibility and about doing the right thing and only YOU can make that decision and only YOU can take care of yourself, through proper nutrition and moderation.

Moderation is the key.

Begin by taking an honest look at yourself making note of changes you would like to make, need to make, and will make to yourself and your lifestyle to make yourself the very best that you can be in all ways.

Now that you've assessed your physical body next you want to look at your soul. Your physical body is *what* you are; your soul is *who* you are. As for your soul we will not go into detail here for that again, is your own personal situation and you as an adult know right from wrong. I strongly recommend in your quest to live a victorious life that you base that quest upon strong moral footing.

We began this book speaking of the lack of meditative state from which this world suffers and the problems created by the lack of personal introspection through quiet solitude.

To be able to plan well and think clearly you must have times of regular mental solitude and this is best achieved through states of prayer and meditation. How you pray or how you meditate is a personal matter for you to decide but again I strongly recommend to you the reader, that effort be made daily by you to set aside time for prayer and or meditation.

This is so important to a successful life in so many ways. You can gain the world but without joy and peace it is worthless.

The next area of assessment that is vital to your success is your mind. Your state of mind and your attitude is the greatest asset you have. The two points of assessment touched upon prior to this, one being the physical body, the other the soul, are the two of the three points of the triad of your being. All must be strong and balanced as a basis for a happy and successful life.

No matter what the threat, no matter what the problem, if you have the right frame of mind backed by a strong soul, combined with health, you are set. Now that we've touched upon the center of the situation, that being *you*, your heart, mind soul and body you must now assess the immediate outward threats that you may face. When I say threats I am not only speaking of major disasters I am talking about all threats you may face.

What are your immediate needs?

We as human beings need three basic things. Those three basic things are food, shelter and clothing. From there our basic needs expand based upon these three. So ask yourself based upon these three basic needs, *near term* what are your needs? Then once you determine your short term needs expand it out further to midterm and then long-term. The best way to do this is to ask a simple question yourself, what if?

What if the power went out?

What if I could not access my funds?

What if the grocery stores were empty?

What if something happened where I could not leave my home?

Taking all of these basic questions apply them all to the three basic needs. The answers you come with are the basis of your plan.

You see, if you bought this book thinking I was going to give you all of the answer you are very wrong.

If I were to attempt to do so it would be in folly, for only *you* can honestly assess *your* true situation and needs. Now your immediate situation after assessment may be of a pressing matter and may be something you need to attend to as quickly as possible.

This could be something economic, this could be a bill that is due or a payment deadline or some other pressing matter that has the potential to disrupt your lifestyle.

Anything that you encounter that you can see as a threat to your wellbeing is to be noted within your assessment and is to be addressed in your plan. This is the purpose of this assessment, to logically list potential threats we may face so we may develop a plan in a logical, thought out manner and then have the plan ready as a contingency.

The goal is to have all needed supplies and items needed to see us through any disruption with relative ease, so that we may continue on with our lives with as little disruption as possible. By doing this and by implementing a plan and by bringing in provision for you and your loved ones, you will find you will greatly increase your peace of mind and when your peace of mind is more stable, your stress and the stress of those around you will greatly diminish. With diminished stress comes increased health which allows a more joyful and full life. Part of being able to do a good and thorough assessment is having the knowledge and awareness of the current events going on around you. Again I will say that "knowledge is power" and you must use this knowledge of current events to aid you in making proper assessment and decisions. During the time of this writing we have access to the Internet and the free flowing form of information it provides, but by the time you read this things may have changed.

If that is the case and you find yourself in a situation where little to no information is being transferred because of disruption or censorship then you must use the method of "outward circles" threat assessment, gathering as much information about what is going on around you and your local community and assess the situation as needed. I would like to add that this situational assessment is always updated by you as needed.

One other thing that must be addressed in your personal assessment is your personal surroundings. We live in a society when many people tend to keep to themselves. The degree to which this is, appears to change region to region, some regions of the world people are very social and reach out to those around them freely. But in many areas people are closed to those around them. The reason for this are varied and really do not matter but what does matter is being aware of who is nearby and what type of persons they may be. I will be covering something in a later chapter that deals with the social interaction that begins during a time of disaster which can result in a disaster of its own...if you do not know *who* you're dealing with. I do not intend to paint this in a negative way, as part of your discovery of *who* may be in your general area you will find many fine people who are an asset to the community. But that is not always the case. Remember the old school wisdom "never judge a book by its cover".

The standard which the world has placed upon success gives a false measure of the person's true worth in a may not be the guide for homes down out of work with the old truck he is always working on who also seems to have a beer in is hand most the day was the problem but it may turn out to be the guy down the road living in the big house and expensive car who is a threat. This is all part of situational assessment, your environment, your economics, the geopolitical situation and your neighborhood and those nearby. These are all things to think about and all things to consider while assessing your situation.

3

Setting Your Goals

Now that you have successfully assessed your situation, you must now categorize the information.

To do so you must take note of all of your listed needs and then place them in order of pressing priority. To do this you must objectively look at all threats and the associated speed that may be needed for resolution or action to deal with each.

First prioritize all needs or resolutions in order of nearest to furthest based upon proximity and time. By now you realize you are producing a *series* of checklist. And this is how it is done, you write a list, you revise a list. You then throw out that list then you make a new list. It is through this ongoing assessment, review and revision process that you get a clear picture of your assessed situation and your needs.

You'll notice as you do this, things will change and the reason for this is because you will naturally refine and eliminate points within your assessment list as you go over things in your mind. And this is a good thing! This is how a haphazard plan evolves into a detailed comprehensive guide! Now, how you do this and exactly in what form is totally up to you.

Some will use legal pads and pens some may use a clipboard; some may use the computer and comprehensive spread-sheets. How it is done does not matter but the amount of thorough detail *does* matter. I would advise that no matter how good your memory, do not try to do this in your mind alone! This task is the type of thing you need to write down on paper and look at. It is the act of writing things out and the ability to leave it aside and come back later to look at it again in freshness that allows for thoughtful revision. One of the primary components or categories on your plan will be "stuff". All of the needed "stuff" and other items you have determined necessary to purchase or acquire to fulfill the needs of your plan. The three basic needs that we have covered before, of food, shelter and clothing will make up the core items on your list but there are also additional *auxiliary needs* that would fall under the categories of health, safety, security and fun. Yes...I said fun. The whole goal of your effort is to produce and activate, a well thought out plan that would allow you and those around you, to continue on with your normal way of life to the best of your ability, with minimal disruption allowing yourself the ability to be happy.

And to be happy one must have fun, so the ability to have fun and to be entertained in stressful situations is very important. This is very important for children as the distraction of games, books and other activities are vital to reducing stress and increasing joy. Now this comes back to the point of your threat assessment beginning at the center. This is the reason I have said a positive attitude is paramount to success. A positive attitude and a good sense of humor in time of duress is worth its weight in gold...or maybe more! Being able to look at any situation head on with a positive, "can do" attitude is vital. Now this positive attitude is not only vital for you but also those around you. Some reading this book may be alone but many have a partner in life, a husband or wife or significant other, and many have children living in your home. And it is in these situations that fear and doubt could cause trouble.

In fact it is common in traumatic situations for those ill prepared psychologically to suffer emotional breakdown. And you'll be required to exhibit strength and calmness in the situation. Now I will add there are some situations that inside your heart and mind as you observe the unfolding events around, you may not feel so strong or calm and it is in these times that it is most important for those around you that you exhibit strength and stability. To do this in some situations requires extensive intestinal fortitude and I might add it is the positive attitude and a good sense of humor that are the basis of this very strength.

You may ask "how can one exhibit a positive attitude and a good sense of humor in a severely traumatic situation?" The answer to that question returns us back to our personal assessment and specifically the topic of your soul. This is why conscious and regular prayer and meditation are so important.

For it is from the strength of your soul, that faith is produced, and it is this faith that must be the solid foundation of your mind. You must "know that you know" all will be well, and to know this requires faith and faith alone. Faith is the foundation upon which all strong and successful individuals stand.

So you have your list, of items, of gear and needs. As I've said before, your personal situation that you find yourself in at this time dictates your actions, your needs and therefore your list of needed items.

Some readers may have the luxury of time and money to carefully gather all that they may need to fill out their list of needed items. Also my list would look nothing like your list as our situations and needs vary from person to person. Yes we have the core basics that we'll build upon and then from that point forward, it becomes varied for the individual.

Some people reading this book will not have the luxury of time but may have money, or may not have the luxury of time and also the disadvantage of little to no money. And all of these factors of course are noted in the assessment and it is because of these variables that resilience and flexibility are needed to effectively deal with any situation.

I have found it helpful that when developing a plan of action to break the items down into categories. Once you have completed your assessment and once you have made a list of your needs you'll see that they have all fallen within the basic categories I laid out before of food, shelter, clothing, health or security.

By separating all of the items into categories you'll find it easier to begin the process of acquiring all needed items. Now again, situation dictates and the process of acquiring your needs could be for one reader at this time just simple shopping online with a credit card or for someone else, driving to local shopping area.

Or your situation may be one more *interesting* and pressing at this time requiring more creative means of provision. We may see a situation during time of infrastructure collapse or failure that the only available means of commerce would be cash transactions only and even in some situations that is impossible.

I have witnessed during power outages all commerce stop! The reason for this is the integration of all the stores with mainframe computers that track all sales and when the power is out, the cash registers stop working. This happened to me not long ago! I was standing in a store and the clerk can rang up an item, had placed the item in a bag and I had my hand extended with a $20.00 bill to hand to the clerk. Right at that moment the power went out...and that was the end of that. I was amazed to find out he could not complete the sale! Even though I had the money in my hand the store could not accept it so I had to walk out of the store empty handed as did dozens of others. And this is the very precarious position we find ourselves in today.

I have often joked that someday, somewhere, someone will trip over an extension cord....and we're all going to die! Now of course that is only a joke but that joke may not be too far from the truth! We are all so dependent upon our fragile electrical grid that if something were to happen to the grid as I touched upon before in the previous chapters that commerce and communication would cease. This is something that should be considered in your threat assessment. This is also one of the reasons (and I will add a big reason) why it is so important to be prepared for disaster or shortfall *before* the need arises.

This goes back to the false sense of security many people have developed because they wrongly think that because of the ample bank accounts they may hold that in the event that something bad were to happen, they would simply go out and buy what they may need then, and only then. Buying what you need when the power is out will not happen...and in fact even getting the money from your account, to buy what you may need when the power is out will *not* happen!

So what we're facing as a society is the eventuality in the future that the ability to conduct normal commerce will cease. After that point in time if the situation continues mid to long term, we will find ourselves in a position where the practice of barter will become commonplace.

Now it is needless to say that the time to prepare is long before we reach that situation and that is what this book is all about, but you may be reading this book after the fact. You may be reading this book by candlelight after the loss of power and if that is the case then so be it. The basic guideline within this book is still valid and workable in *most* cases.

Now that you have all of your needed items or "stuff" categorized you must now lay out goals based upon urgency of need. That urgency can only be determined by you and your current situation.

What I have done in the past is after categorizing and organization of all of my needed items I would mark certain items with the notation of urgency. And of course these are the items to be acquired first by whatever means available. To find and acquire needed items, based upon your threat assessment and level of urgency is your basic goal and is not just one goal but more a series of goals all based upon that one basic question of "what if?" followed by your assessment of your situation.

When setting your goals, limitations both economic and social will be contributing factors.

Can you use your credit card?

Can use your debit card?

Are the stores well stocked?

Are there restrictions or shortages on the items I am looking for?

Will my actions appear suspicious?

This last point is one to consider as we live in an odd time. We live in a society that views personal preparation as eccentric behavior in some ways. This falsehood has been perpetrated by design, by the media and is one issue to be aware of. There is nothing wrong with being prepared for disasters in fact it is the responsible thing to do. But we see a strange anomaly in today's society where on one hand the powers that be encourage preparedness by commercials and public announcements but on the other hand the very same agencies who recommend the public be prepared also put out notices stating that those who prepare may be considered suspicious!

The reason for this is one of control. This creates a situation that people see others who prepare as odd. And this is all done by design. So keeping that in mind if you are reading this and preparing for eventual disaster or shortages in a pre-event world, then you would be a wise to go about your business privately.

Again there is nothing wrong with being prepared but everything wrong with not being prepared. The media has turned everything upside down, what is good is seen as bad what is bad is seen as good and what is wise is seen as *odd*. What was once common in life and common sense for those of balance is now all but lost. Our ancestors knew the fragility of our existence, knew the fragility of our environment and knowing this brought in provision. Most homes today that do have pantries, we find that they are not filled with provisions but are used as a multi-use closet for coats, sports equipment and pet food. The proper use of a pantry was for an area to hold larger amounts of food and staples for use in the kitchen. Beyond that most homes at one time had something called a larder. The larder was a separate area that had even larger amounts of basic staple items that were used to supply the pantry. And then of course there were other storage areas like root cellars and such for the storage of fruits and vegetables. And let us not forget the smokehouse. Many of these terms are alien to most, only being seen in books or in historical tours. This sad fact is a direct result of modern advertising and corporate greed. Corporations know that profits are made from continued sales and to increase sales all efforts must be made to encourage an immediate "must have now" society with a throwaway mind-set. This throwaway mindset has gotten out of hand as we see people so driven psychologically by this media control, that their lust and desire to constantly replace perfectly good items with something "new and improved" is so strong that it overrides common sense and reason. We have an entire industry based upon waste!

People are encouraged to recycle or to donate the excess they may have and with some people this may be a good thing! Many have surrounded themselves with a massive amount of <u>useless</u> items all driven by the psychological desires and impulses placed into their minds by the media. So because of this shift to a "throwaway" society people have become less and less conscious of the wisdom of storing provisions, but are more dependent upon the immediate satisfaction of their desires through the supermarkets, outlet stores and fast food providers all to the increased profits of the corporations. Sad but true.

As soon as you have assessed your situation and have set your goals in a categorized and prioritized way, you are ready to move forward with the initiation of your plan. As you prepare to initiate your plan you must also exercise your personal security and that is best done during this phase by remembering the old school wisdom of "silence is golden".

4

Initiating Your Plan

Now that you have successfully assessed your situation and also set your goals in order it is now time to initiate your plan. Depending upon your situation this could be as simple as Internet shopping or driving out to go shopping at the local shops and stores or it could be a more "interesting" adventure. One of the parts of your plan that I am sure became obvious while setting your goals was the question of logistics and storage. It is one thing to acquire your needed items, it is another to store and protect them well.

There are certain considerations to make about space and environment that we will not go into detail here as there are countless volumes dedicated to the specific topic of "Food Storage". It is very important that your efforts both economic and time wise are not done in vain by improper storage. The obvious factors to consider are environmental extremes of heat, cold and humidity plus the added danger of pest or rodent and when I say rodent I speak of all variety including the two legged. And that brings me again to the point of security achieved through silence.

Remember confidentiality...remembering that silence is golden!

Also along the lines of security you have to remember that if you live in an area where your neighbors can see you as your bring items into your home you need to give this special consideration to not raise suspicion or to advertise to everyone that you have extra food. There may come a time in the near future that your neighbors' knowledge of your storage of extra food could not only be a liability but a potential danger for your own safety. So this security factor of confidentiality should always be a factor in the way you shop, handle yourself and guard yourself on what you say and whom you say it. Many people who are too lazy to take the responsibility to personally prepare for disaster or possible shortcomings of all that is now abundantly available, are all too eager to openly verbalize knowing you are prepared that "they will just come to your house if things get bad!"

Many people think this is a joke...but it is deadly serious. If you think that family and friends with whom you may have shared your concerns with, or maybe even you have gone so far to have shared your plans with, or shown off your provisions to, will not remember about YOUR "stuff" during a time of need...you are greatly mistaken. Many people prepare with plans of helping family or friends and that is fine and noble and if you have the assets to do so that is your choice. But you must know that one of the greatest threats that you can face during totally economic collapse which has resulted in food shortages are not looters....but beggars. For the hardest thing to do is to say "no" to someone in need. You must know that during an economic collapse and the resulting food shortages most all people will be in need.

That fact alone, that most of all people will be hungry and that most all will be in need, could lead to the total undoing of all your preparations in short order by one act of charity after the other.

Who is it you will say no to? Where do you draw the line? What would be the defining factor?

You must also be aware of the fact that one act of misguided charity could announce to all around the very fact that you have extra food and that alone could be your undoing.

40

These are hard things to even think about but is one of the harsh realities that we must face when devising a plan. This topic we will touch upon in greater detail in chapter six of this book which covers security.

Now depending upon your situation and depending upon the result of your personal assessment, the initiation of your plan may begin on different levels. For those whom have discerned the need to address "physical body issues" found during your assessment, part of your plan may include physical exercises or change in diet. If that is the case you may begin you plan by changing your schedule.

This schedule change may include waking earlier in the morning to allowing for time for physical exercise. If that is the case you must remember to schedule time every day for prayer or meditation.

Depending upon your situation and depending upon your surroundings this meditation or prayer could be integrated into your exercise time. Walking or running without the distraction of music can also be a good time for meditative thought. Or even earlier in the morning before you get out of bed. This is a great time to set the tone of the day with prayer and meditation before your feet hit the floor. To consciously contemplate, visualize and plan your day proclaiming to the universe that you're day will be the best that it can be, both proactive and fulfilling for yourself and all around you, being grateful for all the blessings to come your way. That way when your feet hit the floor they do so in victory!

By preparing your mind and heart to have a proactive and successful day, the tasks of the day are made easier. As I have said before, positive attitude and a "can do" spirit are vital for successful and victorious living and by beginning the day with a positive attitude set by meditation and prayer your chances of victory and success are greater in all things!

A major part of initiating a plan is the procurement of your "stuff". And a major part of this is making sound choices. This takes due diligence and study on your part which may involve Internet searches and extensive reading. But if you are currently in an "interesting" situation this could involve looking over goods laid out on a tabletop at local market in a barter situation. Again the actual situation you find yourself in at this time dictates how this is done but the basic principle of finding quality at a good value remains the same. In some situations we may be offered little choice and in those circumstances we take what we can get. But many times we are offered many choices, so many in fact the task could be daunting. This is one of the reasons for taking care in preparation and preparing well before the need arises, so you do not find yourself in a situation with limited choices, limited variety, limited quality or even worse...total shortages. I have found it better to spend a little more if I can, for better quality in most cases. This is very true in foodstuffs. Yes, some things may be much cheaper than others but with that reduction in price many times a reduction of quality and flavor is well pronounced. So much so that you could later have remorse over your purchase and that is never a good thing.

We must remember the whole goal behind "having a plan and plan to act" is to retain our happiness, comfort and joy. If we compromise quality when we can afford not to, it will be regretted later, so this is something to keep in mind while preparing your needed items and provisions. If the situation allows as you're in your plan initiation stage, there are social groups, forms and web sites that can easily be found by Internet search that contain a wealth of knowledge amassed by people who have been preparing for many years and who have reviewed many products. This is a valuable asset when doing your due diligence on the proper items to buy. You will even find suggestions, recipes, tips and tricks on every manner of skill you may need. If you are doing this you want to be sure to not share any personal information with anyone on any Internet site for your own safety and security.

Also it would be wise to avoid any site of heavy political leaning one way or the other. As many of the listeners to my radio show, Phoenix Rising Radio will know I am apolitical or in other words I am a "political atheist" and being so I naturally avoid all such gatherings that focus on political issues, as I see this type of activity to be nothing more than a theatrical display of distraction put forward by the powers that be as a method of control of the masses and therefore more distraction than good.

About shopping....Many of the large club type stores that require membership have good deals on bulk items and some in fact offer online, long-term Food Storage packages. Some of these deals are quite good and offer both the convenience of "to your door" delivery added to the convenience of being able to purchase by credit card online. This is a quick and easy way to bring in your core items that make up the base of your Food Storage. If you have the opportunity to do this you need to keep in mind the storage requirements needed for large bulk items as some of these packages are quite large in their entirety and take up a large space.

This storage question is all part of the basic plan and is something that your situation will dictate. I would suggest in a static location (meaning the location that you will not be moving from or hope to not move from) being your "sanctuary" if you will, that you have your pantry and larder containing your provision located or situated in such a way as to not be obvious or visible to guest or workers if there is a need to enter your home for mechanical service.

I will not suggest a location or storage method as that will be up to you and depends on your home and your location. Just keep in mind as you're planning the amount of space you'll need as you initiate your plan to be able to store all needed food, water and other items.

Water....Water is so important, without water you'll die. Without clean water you'll be sick. Water must be your top priority! During your situational assessment one of the major "what if" questions you should have asked yourself was "what if my water supply were cut off or tainted"?

Being able to effectively store and <u>filter</u> water is so important.

I will not go with into all of the ways and products available for water storage and filtration as there are many. But the topic of clean water for drinking, cooking and personal hygiene should be the highest priority on your threat assessment. Water should be number one on your list and you can begin collecting water for drinking at any time. If you have clean drinking water now you then have water you can begin to store. I will give a few inexpensive tips on water storage. First off never store water in any container that has been used for dairy. One good way to store water is by reusing using two liter soda bottles. Be sure to wash them well with clean water before refilling.

After the bottle is clean you can fill it with your drinking water all the way to the top, and when I say top I mean the *very top*. You must do this slowly as you get near the top of the bottle and carefully bring the water level all the way to the very top to the point it will spill out. Then after filling it to the very top as it is setting up on the counter carefully screw the clean top on to the bottle but just before you tighten it down slightly squeeze the sides of the bottle gently forcing water out the top and as you are doing so tighten down the top. You'll see that when you release the sides of the bottle you have created a vacuum in the bottle and have sealed the water. This bottled water has no air space and if stored well should remain fresh. If you plan to store this water long-term I would suggest doing study on the proper use of chlorine bleach for water purification. This is done by adding 1 to 2 drops from an eyedropper of <u>unscented</u> chlorine bleach into the water as you are filling the bottle.

But again to do this properly you must do your own due diligence as this is a guideline and it is up to you to determine your needs and develop your plan.

One last thing on the topic of water I would like to add is that of <u>flavoring</u>. It is advisable while putting your plan together to add as part of your Food Storage different powdered drink mixes. By doing so it increases the enjoyment and variety that you will have and also is great for masking the taste of some treated waters. Keeping in mind the whole idea of retaining comfort, I would like to say there's nothing like a hot cup of cocoa and piece of hard candy to reduce the stress of the day.

Depending upon your situation and your needs you may have someone helping you and if so that's a good thing as two heads are better than one, and many times our partner will think of things that we forget, or bring up details overlooked. So working together to make sure all needs are met and all areas are addressed is very helpful. But sometimes situation would dictate that the head of a family would do all preparation alone. That could because of work or physical disability suffered by a partner, or other circumstances including child care. If that is the case one must take care when initiating your plan that money is not spent that is not agreed upon. Or that things are purchased that would not be liked, enjoyed or used by your partner and loved ones.

One of the main hindrances you may face could be economic lack. If that is the case then you must do the best that you can do with what you have. One of the biggest assets available at this time, during this writing are so called "Dollar Stores". There are many items that can be purchased for just $1.00 that can be included into your plan. Also for shopping, discount shops, rummage sales as well as "flea markets" can net incredible items for next to nothing. So depending upon your situation and depending upon current availability you will now begin the process of the initiation of your plan.

Go for value, and durability.

Think....before you buy.

5

Avoiding Distraction

We began this book describing the current situation in the world. At the time of the writing of this book, one of great problems is distraction. It seems as if everywhere we go in today's society from the time we wake to the time we go to sleep most are surrounded by a constant din of noise and distraction. Most of this is self-induced and much of it is in fact sought out by the consumer at the great delight of the corporations.

The profits from cell phones, games, movies, music, television and the Internet are astronomical. In some areas of the world it is hard to escape the television screen. Many places in the United States every grocery store line has a flat screen TV. In every aisle in many stores you also find a flat screen TV blaring ads. These televisions blare out a nonstop flow of advertisement and nonsense, nothing but fluff, nothing but brain candy, wrapped in exciting music and flashing images. Many of the gas pumps are also equipped with televisions and as you fill your tank you are subjected to "pump TV" and as you pump your gas the corporations "pump" your mind full of subliminal images! Mindless silliness, reality TV, horrific crime shows, and we even have cop shows with TV cameras showing live arrest. One has to wonder the amount of electronic pollution that we are saturated with. Also what is the effect of all this electronic pollution upon our minds? The result of all of this as I described in the first chapter of this book is nothing less than "mind control by design". Even the wording and phrases used with television are telling. We are subjected to "television programming."

Programming?

Yes, "programming" the very thing you do to a computer. You load in the programs, you enter the data, set the parameters, and you then set up the operating system. And to the delight of the successful programmer if done well, the computer will operate flawlessly, performing all the tasks it is program for. And just like a computer, human beings *also* perform as programmed if the programming has been done in the proper manner. This human programming done for the profits of the corporation is a true science that has been studied and perfected in the laboratory. Careful observation, study and experiments over many years have developed methods of mind control by the use of television. This is not conspiracy theory or speculation this is documented scientific fact. Study has been made in the area of brainwave stimulation by carrier wave, reinforced by audio and visual stimulation. It has been proven that through selective audiovisual stimulation strong emotional response is triggered through the stimulation of certain areas of the brain.

This stimulation not only produces an emotional response, but also a marked chemical release within certain areas of the brain which can induce strong biological urges of rage or lust. But one of the most interesting and valuable abilities of this programming for the corporations is the ability to subliminally implant an almost insatiable desire for *any* product. We're beginning to see the negative results of this type of mental programming upon society.

Just the Christmas season before this writing here in the United States we witnessed riots over the release of a tennis shoe. Just a simple...poorly made.... tennis shoe. The release and issue to the public of this product had been so pumped up on the television with the use of heavy subliminal messaging that

48

the desire and lust for this product was so intense in the minds of the consumer that when the stores opened up on the day that this shoe was made public people went insane. Whatever subliminal messaging that may have been planted into the minds of these hapless victims was so intense things became quickly violent. No one was killed but many were seriously injured and many arrests were made. We also witnessed this same bizarre activity during the 2011 Christmas season. The mind control masters had used the subliminal imaging and advertising of television to program the masses into the most irrational behavior ever witnessed in a shopping season. There were riots, there was violence, people were shot, people were hospitalized, and people went insane like packs of animals clawing over the top of one another like rabid animals tearing at one another for cheap poorly made junk.

Do I really need to say this is not normal behavior?

Is it not obvious that the controllers and media masters have ratcheted up their subliminal messaging and programming to the point that they are pushing the limits? I said in chapter one that in the same way we see the "heavy fruiting tree of tyrannical government" exerting ever expanding controls upon the freedoms of the people, we also see the heavy fruiting of the corporate media mind control masters, pushing the very envelope of subliminal messaging.

So it has gotten to the point of instilling violence in the public during shopping. How much further will they go? How far will they push the envelope? Looking into our matrix of information, based upon historical example they will push it to the limit...and I mean right to the very limit. They will push it to the point that people break. This irrational emotional response that we have seen unleashed this past shopping season will only intensify, as this is the exact desired affect they are going for. For them to witness the public reacting like savage animals as a result of their television programming and subliminal implants is very satisfying to the control masters! To them this is success! This is the desired effect they are going for. They want people to make irrational decisions. They want people to exhibit animalistic lust over cheaply made products. They want people to blindly accept that this is insanity is normal behavior. What they have done they have done well. It is not known what all the exact nature of the carrier waves and subliminal images may be. The question I pulled forward for you the reader is this...Do you really want to know? To truly know the content it would require submitting yourself to it.

My suggestion is to limit the amount of television exposure your mind is subjected too. Yes there's some good viewing on some of the educational channels but you'll see it is also laced with implanted ideas and programming. It would appear that the heaviest of subliminal suggestion and programming is targeted to the broad range of audience that is attracted to a more "brain candy" forms of entertainment such as sitcoms, comedies, reality television and sports. So as far as distractions go television is ranked as number one.

The next distraction we face is music. It seems that we can go nowhere without music being played in our ear...in the car, in stores, in elevators, in offices and in many workplaces. Myself, I like music! And sometimes I listen to the news on radio. But this is always done by me, for my own enjoyment. What I do not enjoy and what is a true distraction, is the other music we are subjected to, some of which has subliminal messaging. This has been well documented and is a big business. In fact the heavy subliminal messaging the public was subjected to before television was the subliminally laced music being pumped through stores and other public places. Within this music that you hear daily in grocery stores offices and other public areas are messages and suggestions, all intended to control your thought process and in turn, control your actions and the primary action induced is first and foremost, is to consume products and the second "suggestion" is to obey all rules and regulations.

Sounds kind of creepy doesn't? That's because it *is* creepy...and all done to control your mind.

So television is one distraction and unwanted radio noise another but what else can be seen as a major distraction in our lives?

One of the big ones is time theft. That's right, time theft. Time theft is what I call the condition that the corporations and large banking institutions have created in most of the world where people are so pressed to make ends meet that most in the household are working many hours and some work two or more jobs. The corporations and banks have effectively stolen our free time! People have become like slaves working from sun up to sundown on the corporate farm just to make below fair wage profits and to then turn those small profits over to the "corporate store" always being a day late and a dollar short, and therefore always remaining in debt in both time and money to the corporate masters. So I list and have ranked the distraction of "time theft" as also being high on the list.

So what to do?

I had one person call in with a question on one of my radio programs and he had a comment on the concept of balance. He shared that he had been working hard to achieve balance through personal spiritual discovery and personal preparation to find both balance and harmony in his life but was having difficulty in finding peace. The caller went on to asked me what is the best way to find this balance...to find this personal peace? And my answer to him is the same solution I put forward to you the reader in this book and that solution is meditation and solitude. The best form and best environment for this is in nature....in the great outdoors. Sometimes your situation will limit your ability to commune with nature and if that is the case then do the best you can do to quiet your environment to the best of your ability. Above all do your best to limit or eliminate television viewing.

Next do your best to control to the best of your ability all other audio distractions. Many times people listen to music and have no idea what the words are saying and sometimes people are shocked to find out what words they've been tapping a foot to. Just because you do not consciously make note of the words of the songs it does not mean you are not subconsciously absorbing it like a sponge soaking up into your mind all type of the adverse and negative audio programing.

To the best of our ability we must limit the amount of entertainment we willingly subject ourselves to. Sometimes we have no choice and are forced to be in an environment because of work or other circumstances that we are subjected to these distractions. But we must consciously and actively do our best to limit the electronic distractions in our lives. We must as responsible human beings take control of the content and information that we take into our minds. It is the responsible thing to do. If possible, the best environment for meditation, relaxation and pure entertainment is in nature. Most of us have access to some form of nature, for some who live in urban areas this access could be a park, for others it may be a nearby wooded area and for some their blessed to live in large park like settings or nearby to one. Either way I encourage everyone to commune with nature to be with the trees, to be near water, to listen to the wind rustling leaves. To look into the clear dark sky and see the stars twinkle and shine like diamonds. There's something about being connected to nature that we have lost as a people. Our ancestors knew the value of the great outdoors, knew the value of the solitude of the wild and the calming effect it had upon the soul.

We in the United States were blessed to have had leaders who came before who saw the value of our natural resources and the beauty contained therein. And seeing this set aside vast regions of natural resource and natural parks to remain guarded and untouched for the benefit and enjoyment of future generations. The harsh contrast we see between the beauty and solitude of nature vs. the constant electronic pollution forced upon us by the corporate media is a stark contrast to be noted.

It is in this natural solitude, even if it is the local park that we can find avoidance of distraction. The natural setting and the connection to the creator that can be made by quiet contemplation in the natural spaces is of such great value to the heart, to the mind and to the body that it should be held in the highest esteem.

This is a pleasure that not only affords beauty for the eye, but provides pleasures for all the senses to the point of having a healing effect. This healing effect if utilized properly by making prayerful connection to the creator through creation, can quickly undue the intentional evil perpetrated upon us by the media programmers.

So by proper identification of the major distractions we face, combined with the knowledge of the healing power of connecting to the creator through creation by literally grounding ourselves to the ground in nature, we're setting ourselves up for total victory, victory through the proper use of knowledge.

To know the threats from distractions and how to counter same is a major part of the battle. More are becoming aware day by day.

By knowing this truth and the importance of breaking free of these distractions you can proactively avoid distractions. By being free from distraction your mind is free to think in a clear concise manner and when you are of clear thought, you can visualize harmony, peace and abundance.

You must see in your mind's eye, both you and those you love surrounded by safety, having all of your needs met. If things get bad, hope for the best and smile.

6

Personal Security

Personal security on all levels...

What do I mean when I say this? Well when I say at all levels
I mean all levels of your existence, all levels of power within
your sphere of existence, all areas around you. In the exact
same way that you determine your threat assessment, by beginning at the center and looking out in concentric circles in a
360° area, is the way that you plan for your personal security.
And just as you began your personal assessment with your
heart, mind and body you do the same with security concerns.
I will say right now that the biggest danger or threat that you
face of immediate danger is yourself. The basis of this threat
I covered in previous chapters, that being, self-doubt, fear,
physical weakness or illness. And those issues we addressed
with a solution of good diet, exercise, prayer and meditation.
Pointing out that the primary healing place for human beings
to regenerate themselves from the harmful effects of electronic mind control is in nature. So working off the premise that
you the reader has successfully assessed, planned for and ini-
tiated the needed steps to correct any defaults observed within
the inner area, known as *yourself* in all forms, heart, mind and
body, this chapter will concentrate on the security needs of
anyone existing during "tumultuous times". The modern
world we live in is an interesting environment that has been
altered by the powers that be in the way described in the previous chapters, altered by electronic mind control for personal
gain and war. Because of this intrusive psychological manipu-

lation and control we have noted the adverse and vile affect it has upon the consumer. But we also face a very dangerous underlying problem that exists like a "sleeping demon" just below the surface of modern society. This "sleeping demon" that I speak of are the yet unseen changes both morally and psychologically of the masses as the result of gaming. Gaming is a big business...one that brings in billions of dollars yearly and is valued at over sixty five billion dollars for the entertainment industry! That is big money! Anytime we see big corporate money we see big corporate greed and big corporate greed will do *anything* they can to manipulate the minds of the consumer to make them mindlessly consume more to just to increase their profits. This blatant greed which uses the mind control system we have described in this book has perfected this in the gaming platform. Even in the simple, seemingly mundane and nonviolent games we have seen negative societal ramifications reported in the past by the press but we do not see a lot of this reported as the press are owned by the corporate giants who are the very ones who profit from this control over the minds of the masses. We have seen reports of child neglect by parents who have been so taken in by the psychological power of these games that the children were reduced to starvation and squalor, as the parents are driven to the verge of insanity, no longer caring for the well-being of their own children. The parent...becoming psychologically manipulated into an obsessed state, of controlled lust, caring of only getting to the next level of the game that they are trapped in. I do not use the word "trapped" lightly for it is nothing less than a trap.

Psychological manipulation in gaming is so strong because of the subliminal triggers and implanted keys within the programming of the game causing the hapless victims to become psychologically trapped. When they're not playing the game they daydream about the game. They spend hours of free time thinking about their next gaming session.

This obsession created by the psychological manipulation has ruined relationships, has cause people to fail in school and has in fact caused people to lose employment. This is just the obvious and notable effects of gaming seen on the surface at this time. When I speak of the "sleeping demon" below the surface, I speak of the changes that have been programmed deep within the psyche of the population by the obsession with the violent gaming. Some of the games that are most popular are extremely violent. We have large gaming communities that are continually waging violent warfare online nonstop. We have teenagers, adults, all forms of society while home at night and weekends wasting free time to transform themselves into killing machines. The primary goal of the game is to win, but to win the game you must kill and not only kill but kill in the most violent way. This constant repetition of killing and the psychological programming that is being done in mass to the population poses a great danger to society in the event of societal breakdown. For it will be then that we see under the duress and stress of fear, lack and uncertainty the breakdown of moral barrier within individuals. It is this very thin moral barrier that separates and prevents the subconsciously implanted, programmed behavior, of murder and mayhem (which has become like a second reality for most of the population) from erupting in real time. I point this out as a great danger and this is something we all must be aware of. There have been movies made in the past about mind controlled sleeper agents. In these fictitious stories we see depicted soldiers or perhaps random people kidnapped against their will who are then subjected to what is called "brainwashing". This brainwashing is achieved by the forced subjection of nonstop violent images and sounds during which time the subject is loaded with psychological triggers that will be activated by keywords or sounds at a later time by the will of the controllers.

I think by now you are beginning to realize this is indeed not a fiction but a terrifying reality within modern society, is a danger that we all now face....the "sleeping demon".

As part of my training one of the interesting things I learned was that during time of disaster there is a basic psychological pattern that human beings follow. The interesting thing about this is that this pattern appears to replicate itself no matter where in the world the disaster may strike or what people groups may be involved. The basic human nature and the basic human reaction to certain stimuli, good or bad, appear to have a universal nature. An interesting pattern of behavior of humans in stressful situations is one that develops during a time of disaster and is pattern I will explain at this time.

Disaster strikes: Day 1

It has been observed and well noted that when disaster strikes human beings on the first day are concerned mostly with themselves and their immediate family doing the best they can to contact those emotionally close to them.

During this first day, a slight sense of unease and agitation begins. The cause of this unease is exasperated by the sudden inconvenience of infrastructure interference, be it the loss of electrical power, phone service or other basic services. As day 1 goes on the feeling of unease builds and the stress and fear levels rise.

Day 2

On the second day of continued disruption people switch their focus from themselves and their immediate family to those in the neighborhood around them. You'll see people venture out more making contact with those in their immediate vicinity. They will speak with neighbors and form small groups. From the small groups you'll see a sense of community spirit arise. People begin to reach out in a benevolent way seeking to com-fort and aid those in need. This second is the day that people check on the old woman down the street who no one has seen for a couple days, this is the day when people share things with one another; this is the day when the community spirit of anger over the current situation begins to rise. Also on the second day is when the parties start. The second day is the day of communal spirit, optimism and the start of collective anger, a low level of anger but anger still. At the end of the second day everyone is sure that resolution of the situation is near at hand. This feeling of pending resolution is the result of the communal outreach and benevolence exhibited and witnessed by all during this second day and all go to bed with more hope and higher expectation of resolution of the situation by the next day.

Day 3

On the third day things begin to change.

This change happens as people begin to wake and begin to assess what is going on around them. Finding that the disaster situation with continued infrastructure interruptions has not been resolved but is ongoing, people begin on the third day to quickly fill with anxiety. This anxiety begins to slowly exhibit itself socially with violence and looting. This is why you see the concentration of effort from the powers that be and they that control to tout the "three day" emergency supply kits recommended for disaster preparation. It is known that if the population has at least a three day supply of needed items it will prevent or extend the noted "third day" effect.

Now in an extended situation as has been seen in the past in a few of the recent major natural disasters the "three day kits" recommended by government agencies would do nothing but extend the inevitable. The inevitable I speak of is the result of the psychological breakdown within the population immediately affected by the disaster. In the best of times and the best of situations before the violent subliminal programming began, the potential and inevitable factor of violence and violent acts that appear on and after the "third day" were not as pronounced but we're still noted, as this is the basic pattern of human behavior. If you have the opportunity in your local community you can observe this phenomenon for yourself.

Knowing of these basic patterns can give you an edge and aid you in your personal security measures during a time of disaster. The reason I have pointed out the issue of the "sleeping demon" of violence subliminally placed into the minds of the masses is to make you aware of the type of situation you could potentially face in the event of societal collapse. Desperate people do desperate things and desperate people who have been subliminally programmed to kill and subliminally programmed to think that in a survival situation the only way for them to survive and the only way for them to get what they want is by extreme violence is a situation we must be aware of.

During times of disaster or societal collapse basic services are stressed or nonexistent and in the worst of cases it becomes an "every man for himself" atmosphere. This was witnessed during the hurricane Katrina event. Many of the police officers who were called and tasked with con-trolling violence and looting during the Katrina event just went home! They had their own families to care for and did not have the time or the desire to perform their duties.

60

So if you combined the "sleeping demon" with the specter of no police forces then add in hunger, fear and desperation you end up with nothing less than the potential that you may have to prevent and stop desperate people from harming you to get your stuff.

We have seen in this country the Center for Disease Control, the CDC put out warnings of a pending "Zombie Apocalypse". This campaign warning of the zombie apocalypse and how people should prepare for the breakdown of all society during the event was said to have been done in jest just to get the public's attention. I will say again many a truth is said in jest.

Zombie apocalypse... I would say that sums it up well as the definition of a zombie is the walking, living dead, who killed to feed off of the living.

I would like to add that the whole thought of society breaking down to such a point is a concept you must keep in balance and not allow cause fear. It is just a factual reality of the human existence, human nature and the inevitable process that has happened repeatedly throughout history in many societies. So it is paramount that you keep your mind balanced and strong in all of this never allowing fear to steal your joy. Now that may sound like a mighty task and for those unprepared and for those taken by distraction it would be. But for you, having assessed the situation and having planned for this situation you can not only override the fear, but you can protect yourself and those you love against the "Zombie Apocalypse" threat situation. And that....is the goal of this book, for indeed a zombie apocalypse would be a tumultuous situation and this is a guide for successful, victorious living in tumultuous times...zombie apocalypse included.

Up to this point I have mentioned many of the contributing factors that would amplify the negative emotional response of a population during the stress of a prolonged disaster but one of the contributing factors I have not included and will indeed be a major factor will be the conditions created because of the greed of the pharmaceutical giants. A major point of concern is the devastating results and effects that we will witness in the population as the result of the sudden discontinuation, due to shortages or supply interruption, of all psychotropic medication. All of the medications that are pushed and prescribed as an anti-anxiety, anti-depressant and even the medications for people who are antisocial are consumed and used at this time by one in five of every persons in the United States. It has been revealed and it is one of the warnings (one of the many warnings I will add) that the sudden discontinuation of the use of many of these medications can have severe adverse effects which can include illness, death and also violent outburst. So we can throw that troubling aspect into the mix with the rest.

Are you starting to get the picture here?

The need for personal security on all levels at all times is paramount. To stay happy and to stay healthy you must feel and be safe. There are countless volumes on personal safety that go into all of the details and training you may need. I'm going to point out the major areas to cover in your personal planning. As noted before the first area being that is nearest to you is your heart, mind, soul and body. The next area that many overlook when covering security is one that directly affects your heart, mind, soul and body and the wellbeing of your existence and that is your money. For without money or a means of exchange your basic needs will be difficult to meet. There may come a time when all means of exchange other than barter will be worthless. You've heard said by some that "you can't eat gold" that is true but at this time you can con-

62

vert gold to "stuff" As we are looking at the inevitability of societal failure and economic failure due to a war or natural disasters how do we protect ourselves in all situations economically? I am not qualified in any way to give financial advice and if I were, I would not. But what I will do is remind you that I suggest balance in all things. Perhaps one of the greatest things you can do to protect yourself is to exhibit and practice balance economically. Now when something is balanced it is not all one sided but instead it is spread out equally as to not be too heavy on one side or the other. When one looks at the basic economic reality of modern society we see a great imbalance. We have different forms of money and wealth. One being electronic held as electronic digits within banking computer systems the other being cash money. We all know that if the electronic infrastructure fails the banking computers go down as do the ATMs as do most point of purchase for retail outlets. It has been observed that during some electronic disruption often times there'll be a few stores, mostly of the mom and pop variety, who will continue to do business by candlelight or lantern but only accepting cash. The problem faced by most people is that all of their money is being held electronically by the banks and most are caught with little to no cash at the onset of disaster. This problem is the result lack of balance plain and simple.

So how would one correct this lack of balance?

The obvious solution would be to always have cash on hand in secure location. But let's take this balance equation further. We touched upon earlier in this book the negative effects upon a nation's economy and currency during time of warfare, particularly if that nation is on the losing side. During economic disaster or duress you can witness your nation's currency become worthless or near worthless overnight. There are many historical examples of this in the last century and the disruptive psychological as well as physical affect upon the population is always extremely negative. So what to do? If you have achieved balance in your personal finances protecting yourself from the inevitable problems resulting from electronic failure how do you protect your physical currency from the possibility of loss of value? The answer to that would be to purchase and own precious metals, gold and silver.

Gold is fascinating. It has been a reserve of wealth for thousands of years. One of the interesting aspects of gold is its universal recognition as a store of wealth. Consider this interesting example: If you had access to a time machine and you could use that time machine to go anywhere on earth, anywhere in time in the past and took with you on your time travels one gold coin, no matter where or when you would travel back to, you could use that one gold coin to buy "stuff". I find that thought fascinating. Now will gold always have worth? The matrix of information tells me the answer to that is no. Because in the worst of times where all economy has failed and all commerce has failed in that situation gold will have little to no value other than beauty. But until that time gold and silver coin are a method of economic balance and safety. If you decide to balance your economic security in this method by the purchase of gold and silver coin, due diligence is required.

It would also be well to note that expensive numismatic gold and silver coins will lose all numismatic value during time of crisis and will only be worth in a barter situation their weight in gold and silver which means the smart choice when attempting to achieve economic balance and security in the potential of economic collapse is to purchase and own non numismatic bullion coins. Again due diligence is required and let the buyer beware. This brings us to our next and a very important security consideration and that is privacy. Personal privacy is one of the most important proactive security measures you can deploy. Many victims of crime have become victims by simply saying the wrong thing to the wrong person. Self-control and more so the control of the tongue is the most important security skill you must learn. This need of confidentiality should be obvious after discussing economic balance and how to achieve same. Many victims of robbery have later been heard to regret simple conversations they may have had with a friend or acquaintance. Most robberies and home intrusions are perpetrated by persons known by the victims. People sometimes wrongly trust family members or friends with private and personal information, private and personal information that should never be shared. Why do they do this? Many times it is done out of pride...pride of ownership of something of great value such as beautiful gold and silver coins or other things of great value.

You may have made the connection by now that this failing, points right back to the center of the security of your heart and mind. If a person violates their own security by revealing confidential information about ownership of something of great value and they have may have done so because of pride. If done out of pride they may have done so because of being out of balance within their own heart and mind. This is why personal prayer and meditation are so important! We must guard our thoughts for if our thoughts are not controlled then our actions and words will not be measured and that can lead to devastating consequences. One of the most important aspects of personal security is the ability for you and those around you to retain confidential information. Many times this requires the withholding of confidential information from family members. I do not advise in any way that you withhold any information from your partner as the bond of trust and love are paramount, but what I am saying is that in some instances most notably in the case of children it is highly advisable to not share any vital information about anything of great value in your possession. Children like to talk, children like to brag, it is one of the traits of childhood and unfortunately many adults retain this childlike trait. So silence...is golden...silence is key.

The other basics of personal security that many overlook are those of noise and light discipline. I will also add to this the need to be conscious of cooking aroma.

If you are in a location that you have made secure by proper planning and you have done your very best to initiate your plan and to bring in provision to see you through time of lack and you have cautiously guarded your words exercising diligence and discretion, that can be all be undone by not observing noise, light and aroma discipline. You may have included in your plans something such as a generator and the means to operate this generator with provision of fuel. In a time of disaster beyond the "day three" threshold you'll now know that you will have desperate people searching out for provision. Things like generators and other equipment make a lot of noise. This is something to take into consideration and there may be times when running a generator and the sound it produces could be detrimental to your security. Also other loud sounds can also be heard long distances after the distraction of music, cell phone and automobiles has long ceased. Anything that produces loud sounds such as mechanical engine noises or other noise producing items must be considered and must be covered in your security plan. Be creative and put some thought to this and I'm sure solutions will come.

Next you must address light discipline. Light discipline is the act of carefully preventing light from being seen from your home during darkness by anyone outside of your safe place. This is a consideration because light can alert others of your location from a distance. You would be amazed how far a single candle can be seen on a clear dark night!

During time of power outages to prevent unwanted attention to your home it is best to observe strict light discipline. There are many ways to do this but a simple one is to just be prepared to cover your windows from the inside so no light escapes. Be creative and test a few methods. This was a common practice during world war two with the use of "blackout curtains". Blackout curtains were heavy black curtains that were placed over all windows at night to prevent any light from escaping therefore preventing enemy bomber crews from seeing the urban landscape below. One simple solution if available to you at the time of this writing is to use heavy duty black contractor grade, garbage bags. These are handy items to have around as they can be used for storage if needed and of course for the disposal of waste but also make a fine blackout curtain. These black bags are large and cover most windows and can be simply taped in place over the windows as needed. They can be easily removed, easily reused or can also function as a barrier when "sheltering in place". This use of blackout curtains and by being careful by not using bright lights outside at night, if you think someone may be near, will go a long way in protecting and securing your location from detection. I mentioned cooking aromas; again you would be surprised in the right conditions how far the aroma of cooking food can travel. Now in many cases there is not a lot we can do about this if we are forced to cook outside, just be wise about what you do and how you do it and think about the ramifications in your personal situation. The cooking of food during time of need has also been flaunted as a thing of pride by those who do not exhibit sound balance. To keep this in perspective remember that starving people are desperate people and the base animal response that can be triggered by the smell of delicious cooking food within the minds of the desperate is indeed a dangerous situation. You better think about that. When describing light discipline I mentioned that when covering the windows with the heavy duty black bags that this can serve as a dual use of light discipline and as a barrier during a "shelter in place" situation. "Sheltering in place" is a term used for a way to protect your home from the harmful effects of environmental dangers in the air. The proper way to shelter in place is to make sure all equipment used to heat and cool your home that may bring fresh air in from the outside are turned off and that all windows and doors are sealed with plastic and tape to prevent harmful vapors from entering your home. The primary supplies used for this are duct tape and plastic. And as I said before the very black bags used as blackout curtains can also serve as the shelter in place vapor barrier. There are considerations to keep in mind and safety concerns to be observed, the primary one being carbon monoxide poisoning. This can happen by the improper use of heating or cooking devices in a home that has been sealed using the shelter in place guidelines. Fresh air and fresh water are vital to your health and survival and being aware of your air quality at all times both inside and out is important part of your security awareness. When most people think about personal security the first thing that comes to mind are weapons and methods of self-defense. I will not go into the details of all the different types of weapons and means of self-defense as that will be covered in great detail in the future by myself in an upcoming book. But for the purpose of this book when addressing personal protection you must evaluate your personal needs along with any legalities and or restrictions you may face by imposed governmental ordinances. Also you must determine exactly what your needs are and parameters of the space you will need to defend. Again going to our concentric circles of security starting in close, design your personal protection choices based upon closest to furthest away. Also remember noise and light discipline and do not dismiss the value of the simple. A personal defense weapon can be a simple walking stick or some other multi use item. That of course is the most simple and close in and not something I would take to a "zombie apocalypse" by choice and your choices made in this matter are vital and key.

When evaluating your security needs proper training and knowledge of the tools you choose are vital. For without proper training a deadly weapon can be deadly to you. Also do not overlook nonlethal weapons and nonlethal methods available to you as many times this form of protection would be the one most needed. Often times the mere show of force of brandishing a weapon is enough of a psychological deterrent to turn away those of ill intent. But that is not always the case. As stated before in my description of the "sleeping demon" there is a false "psyche" that has been formed in many, a sense of false bravery" that is destined to push the foolish and brash into bold aggressions thinking little of the true consequences. It is for this reason I will now mention a bit of old school wisdom and that is to "never a judge a book by its cover". Know this; the sleeping demons will not be in uniform, the sleeping demons will not be of one size, race or sex. The sleeping demon may appear at first glance to be weak and unthreatening but know this...below the surface dwells a twisted psyche, a psyche that has been trained and implanted over hundreds of hours to know one thing and one thing alone, and that is to win at all cost, and to win, you must kill.

I would like to conclude this section on personal security by stressing the importance of proper training and use of weapons. Deadly weapons are just that, deadly. And proper training and practice is vital. Your choice of weapons should also include consideration about the use of these weapons for hunting if needed. It is always good to be sure all items if possible have multiple uses. Not all items can have multiple uses and some are very specific. But do your best to consider durability, functionality and your ability to repair and replace parts as needed. Many times you will find that the simpler something is the more durable it is and therefore more dependable and in an extended time of social turmoil dependability and reliability will be found to be of great value. Again I will say that your personal security begins with your state of mind. Knowledge is power and in this case, the knowledge and skill of the proper use and proper deployment of weapons of defense is paramount. If you are so blessed at the reading of this book, to be in a peaceful, non-disrupted society, with infra-structure and economy intact you would be wise to use this time to learn as much about as many varied practical skills that you can. Now is the time is to power up with knowledge and skills.

Again, remember that your body and health also need defending from sickness and disease so nutrition, rest and exercise form the basis of all of your physical security.

Now is the time.

7

Contingency Plans

So you have made your assessment, you have developed a plan and you have begun to initiate your plan. But what do you do if things change? That is where the contingency plan comes into play. A contingency plan is a backup plan, in the event things change. Having a contingency plan is smart in any situation and is part of successful living. In fact all of the points brought up in this book and the guideline laid forth are practical in any situation we face, as the basic mechanics of having a plan and planning to act in all situations, be it mundane or "interesting".

The way to develop a good contingency plan is by the use of the one tool we began this book with and that is the question of "what if." That is how it is done. After you have developed your plan and you begin working over the separate sections and parts of your plan always inject the "what if" question. By doing this you can see the weaknesses of your plan and the need of alternate ideas or methods if needed. This is how you work out your contingency plans. This must be done in a method of balance and you must remember that there can only be so many preset contingencies. But having an alternate plan of action in any situation is a wise thing.

This is a common military practice and is part of every effective military plan. To give example, say if you plan one route to a destination it is wise to have a contingency of a second route in the event that the primary route is impassible. Likewise you would do the same for your exit route. And you can do this in all parts your life at all times. What if your current form of income would stop? What's the contingency plan? What if the planned route to a safe area in the event of disaster were blocked? What is your contingency plan? What if the "stuff" you have collected became damaged or stolen? What's the contingency plan? Now I will warn you that contingency planning is not for the obsessive! If you're prone to over thinking and over analyzing situations then let the planner beware! We can only plan for so many things and we cannot plan for everything, this is why mindset and attitude are so important and I will guarantee you that in the event that you have to institute a contingency plan a strong disposition and a good sense of humor are handy to have. Sometimes things happen that are so beyond our control there's nothing we can do and no matter how extensive the planning, or how many or complete the contingencies we have it will just not matter. And in that case, strength of heart, mind and soul will be your fortress. And it is in this fortress of the heart where the ultimate peace and safety are found. Having and making contingency plans if done correctly becomes a way of life. And not something that is obsessed over but a simple matter of fact. This comes easy for some who have gone through military training as part of good military training is to always have a contingency plan. Always try to be observant of your environment and your surroundings no matter where you may be. One example might be a shopping area filled with busy shoppers, as you enter and move about the shopping area take note of the location of exits and always keep in mind the direction and distance of all closest known or observed exits. Stay aware of environmental conditions and weather.

And in the event of unexpected violent weather make note of where to take shelter. These are all examples of day to day methods of planning contingencies. This is all as simple as being observant, conscious and aware of your surroundings while also actively asking the question of "what if." As I said this is not for the obsessive and it could easily become an obsessive compulsion for those so inclined. Again balance is required in all things, contingency planning included! Contingency planning and having contingencies extends to having redundancies and replacements for vital equipment and tools.

Some of the things that we all take for granted are all items to be considered for redundancy. At the time of this writing there are many things we take for granted that would almost be impossible to obtain during time of shortages.

Items to look at to possibly have backups and replacement for are those items that would be difficult to replicate and that are vital to your health, safety and happiness. Some of these items might include reading glasses, dental devices and items of comfort. Items of comfort will be a big deal because it will be the simple pleasures and com-forts that we will most enjoy. For the whole purpose of having a plan and planning to act is that we may be happy and joyous to the best of our ability in difficult times.

Simple pleasures and the simple comforts they can bring cannot be overstated for aid helping relieve stress during stressful times. Many of these comfort items you may determine require redundancy or backup, at the time of this writing can be found relatively cheaply and abundant.

A vital part of your economic contingency should be planning for a possible barter economy. What type of items could you purchase now that could be used for barter items in the future?

This question is best answered by you, as your area, and the needs and likes of those around you may dictate the items. There are some common items that would be in great need everywhere and would be of value in any barter situation but in some because of cultural differences some specialty or comfort items might be very specific to your area. Also as part of your contingency plans if applicable in your area garden seeds could be a valuable addition for personal use or barter.

One of the points of the economic contingency, I would like to say is to having a backup in the event of investment failure. It has been speculated and warned by many that we could see a total breakdown of failure of full paper type investments in the world. When I say paper type investments I am referring to 401 K's, certificates of deposit, annuities, stocks and bonds. This includes in the investment you may have that is not the tangible asset but only in electronic digits. The very fragility of our system which could lead to the breakdown of our infrastructure on a long-term basis would make all paperback assets if unavailable. ·

Also currency investments that you may have no matter what currency it may be is also at risk. Nations rise in nations fall and this can happen quickly, quicker than most realize. So if you are holding the currency as an investment you must have a contingency in the event something were to happen on geopolitical level that would cause that currency to become worthless. This is something to consider and this is one more reason to have contingencies for your economic situation.

We saw situation in the nation of Iraq during wartime where no one was paid. And during this time it was not active warfare on a large scale but more of an insurgent uprising.

Life still went and people still went to work but many people did I get paid! Even the police forces, military and government workers were not being paid sometimes for months! The reason for this was the cause of all of the disruptions to the electronic banking system and infrastructure. The situation was exasperated by the near worthless local currency all due to the geopolitical turmoil. Any nation can face such a crisis and to think that your nation cannot is folly.

So very important part of your contingency planning must be asking yourself the question of what if my investments were to fail?

The general idea of contingency plans and having backups should be applied to all of your planning as well as the assessment of your gear.

Having backups for your back-ups and plans for your plans is the general theme and method of successful contingency planning with ease. This is the part of your planning that is ongoing with the adjusting, the tweaking and revising to add to your pro-visions. Checking for freshness in storage food, checking batteries and the occasional inspection of your "stuff" is mandatory.

The primary goal is to not need the contingency plan is avoidable and many times simple care and cleaning of your things goes a long way in extending the life of your gear.

A good rule to remember is that if you take care of your gear your gear will take care of you!

One thing you must watch out for and that is never store batteries in an item long term. They will leak out and can ruin your equipment. And rust and mildew will ruin things fast! Proper storage of gear is needed and we will go into great detail on the aspect of proper storage in the next volume but many very good articles can be found on the internet that give good solid information on the proper storage of most any item long term.

The best contingency plan is the one you never have to use and just remember that spares and extras can also be used in a barter situation if needed.

Bottom line...always remember to check freshness and replace items as needed! This is all done on a continued basis as a means of improving your plans and therefore increasing your probability of successful, victorious living in tumultuous times by the practical application of contingency plans that are functional, flexible and practical in all things, be it a zombie apocalypse, an unstable job market or a trip to the mall, which some may say is no different than the zombie apocalypse!

8

Having Fun!

The primary goal of "having a plan and planning to act" is that we may live a full, pleasurable, enjoyable life even during difficult, trying and tumultuous times. And to do so one of your primary goals that you must remember is to always have fun! For without fun and joy, what purpose does life hold?

We have not come into this life to suffer, even though some would think so. Yes it is true we go through life and we learn lessons and sometimes these lessons bring with them great hardship as part of the learning process and part of emotional and spiritual growth but one of the primary lessons to be learned in life is that we must seek out the good in all things. This goes back to the very core of your assessment. This goes back to the very core of our readiness. This very core and foundation of your strength is your heart, mind and soul. I speak often of balance and stability and in the midst of turmoil and in the midst of hardship I can think of nothing more valuable to bring balance to the situations then the ability and skill of having fun.

Now when thinking about fun what I am referring to is the pleasure and enjoyment that you attain from the different activities you partake in.

Many people being controlled by the media take lavish vacations or do expensive activities that do nothing more than induce great stress. How many times have you come home from a vacation or trip with a feeling of disappointment, tiredness and regret?

Now it is not always so, sometimes there are getaways and vacations that we hate to leave! Simple pleasures you have tapped into that bring you great joy. What I speak of are pumped up trips and pumped up destinations that are pushed upon the populace for profit by the corporations. It is this induced thought pushed upon on your mind that if you do this expensive thing, in this expensive place, you will be loved by your children or loved by your spouse or you'll find love or some other such implanted suggestion. When someone falls for such marketing many times it is followed by both the draining of the emotions as well as the bank account.

What we will concentrate on here are the simple pleasures in life for I have found that in life the simple pleasures are the best of pleasures. During my life I have been blessed with and in interesting career and during this interesting career I've encountered people of great wealth. One would think that people of great wealth are people of great joy but that could not be further from the truth. Many times we have read the sad news about someone of great fame meeting a tragic end because of drug abuse, or suicide. Oftentimes the public is shocked at the news because to all appearances the person looked happy. How can this be that someone who appears to have little to worry about, who appears to have the world in their hand, would become so grieved to take their own life? This is evidence of the great truth that money cannot buy happiness. It is this great deception that is part of the media onslaught of lies and control. You've heard said, that money changes people and sometimes that is true but many times it is not so much the change within the person but more so the changes of those around them. The combination of the false expectations people hold that having wealth always brings happiness added to societal and social pressures, of those around them drives many persons of great wealth into a miserable existence. This is not always the case and in fact there are many people of great wealth I have encountered who very happy and very balanced. And the interesting thing I have noticed is that the happiest people with the greatest wealth are those who enjoy the simple pleasures of life. Not all of them had always been happy and many of them through much pain and suffering and seeking answers discovered the truth after much time. After much time and after much money spent! Money spent chasing happiness, happiness that was always temporary, happiness that was always fleeting, happiness that always seem to be one more expensive activity or destination away. The lucky ones who discovered how to find peace and happiness that is lasting and fulfilling were very pleasant people to be around but the others existed in turmoil and strife being never satisfied.

The interesting observation that I made was that the simple pleasures that brought the greatest happiness to those of great wealth often times was nothing more than a rediscovery of what brought them joy in their childhood! Many of the pleasures were things such as gardening, cooking, crafts of all sorts and outdoor activities such as hiking, camping, fishing, bird watching and star gazing.

You'll notice that these activities that brought to these very wealthy people great joy are activities available to most all. Many of these activities can be done with little to no money and many of these activities can be enjoyed in most areas no matter where on earth. These are the things that bring simple joy and satisfaction. These are things that are fun!

So when thinking about having fun in the context of this book you must start with the "what if" question.

And in doing so you'll find that most of the simple activities are non-reliant on infrastructure or services and in fact are many activities that might become vital to daily existence.

The goal of all of this is to meld your planning and your initiation of your plan into something fun. One way to do this is to begin honing your skills and improving your training and ability by doing fun activities. Hiking and many other outdoor activities are good exercise and also give us the opportunity to experience nature with all of its healing properties. Other activities that are fun are gardening, landscaping and learning about herbs.

You can sharpen your skills with archery, marksmanship and other outdoor craft. One great hobby and fun thing to do which greatly adds to your knowledge base and is highly advisable is to learn the lost an ancient ways. The skills that American native and other indigenous peoples commonly used on a day to day basis are skills that are fun to, learn useful to know, skills that you could pass on to others and foremost knowledge that should be preserved. Many of these loss ways are incredibly ingenious and simple. There are many books and resources on the subject and you may find if you look a local historical group in your area or a reenactment group or club that would be a wealth of knowledge to tap into. Many people who have the skills enjoy sharing them with others freely. Much of the knowledge of these ancient ways can be found during the time of this writing on the Internet. If you are so blessed to be reading this pre event I would encourage you to power up with this knowledge immediately.

Learning something new is always fun but to retain the knowledge takes practice and it is through this active practice of the learned skills we experience fun.

I mentioned gardening and cooking. These activities go hand in hand and can bring great joy and fun.

What good is it if you store flour in your pantry but do not know how to use it? Activities like a learning to bake bread in its simplest form can bring great joy. I will say that the best tasting bread that you'll ever eat is the bread made by your own hands!

The satisfaction of planting seed, tending to and growing vegetables and then enjoying the bounty of your garden on your own table is great!

The sweetest fruit I have ever eaten has been from the trees planted by my own hand. Now was that fruit truly the sweetest? To me it was without a doubt.

Hunters and fishermen know this joy and satisfaction received from preparing meals of their own provision.

There is much that we can learn that will aid us in living a happy life. But you must remember the "can do" attitude that you develop and strengthen through your prayer and meditation for it is this "can do" attitude that gives you success in all that you set your hand to.

Are all things easy to do? Are all things easy to learn? Of course not, it is this challenge at times that is fun. So finding skills that may be needed and learning the skills and practicing those skills can be great fun.

One of the aspects of learning new skills, is that to your friends or family, your activity is an easily explainable "hobby". Also many fun skills and activities can be done with our family or friends. This greatly increases the fun factor as well as increases the core knowledge base. All of the above mentioned activities and skills are so varied that most should find an activity that will bring great personal satisfaction and joy.

There are many activities that I enjoy and consider great fun which began as an exercise in learning. Many of my friends also enjoy activities that fit in with planning, training and learning of skills.

One of my friends constructed a smokehouse and has a great time smoking meat and enjoying the final product. I also have one friend who enjoys woodworking and his skills are extended to the use of non-electric hand tools.

I might add this is a great skill to learn and non-electric hand tools are must have items in the non-electric world. Learning the proper and skilled use of non-electric tools is great fun. The satisfaction and joy brought by constructing something by your own hands is great. When you start it may be a challenge but within that challenge is the fun.

Many of the skills and activities described above can be seen as a form of art and if done well with passion truly is artistry. But art itself is a skill in its own and can be a pleasurable pastime for all. Learning to use the natural elements found in nature for your art is also enjoyable. Art is as old as mankind and some of the greatest works of art ever seen by this world were conceived and produced centuries before the advent of electricity. So logic would say that during a period of electric disruption the production of beautiful art could be prolific. So be sure to gather your art supplies and have fun.

One of the great forms of art is music and music is as old as mankind. If you play an instrument now you might want to make provision to be to ensure you'll be able to enjoy your instrument well into the future.

Many instruments were handmade and learning to make instruments by hand is a skill in its own right and can be seen as a great and valuable skill now and in the future and would be one thing to consider if you are pondering what type of fun activity to pursue.

The subjects that we're covering in this section and the discussion of learning these fun skills while enhancing our knowledge base has an added bonus that should not be overlooked and that being the economic value of your learned skill and the resulting products of same. To learn a skill of value and to learn to produce basic items of need and value is to learn to be self-sustaining in many ways. The skills and resulting products can be used in any barter economy as a form of commerce. To be of value to yourself, those you love as well as the community is a good thing and something to consider.

What about other fun things? Remembering the potential for the loss of electrical grid we must think of other ways to stimulate and occupy the mind in a fun way while inside homes. Many of the activities and games that have been enjoyed for centuries have all but gone by the wayside being replaced by the electronic onslaught mentioned before.

These activities and games that would bring both fun and intellectual stimulation which gives both healthy distraction and stress reduction are all items you need to include in your plan.

During extended time periods of being inside, which could be because of security or environmental reasons such as snow, rain, environmental pollution or other reasons games are a must!

Many of these games that have survived centuries have been found in the tombs of the pharaoh's. They were placed there because they were known to be of great value to the owners bringing great pleasure and satisfaction. Some of these games are easy to reproduce with limited supplies but during the time of this writing, board games are freely available and inexpensive. Nice games of quality and simplicity also make fine barter items. It is best to stick with the simple and classic games as they have been proven by the test of time. Some of the basics being chess, checkers, Chinese checkers, dominoes, mah jong, man-cala, backgammon, decks of cards and dice. There are others that you can look into and you may have your favorites. The other thing to consider on the subject of fun, are toys and sports items. Again stick with the simple stuff, things that are simple, durable and if you need to you could make replacements. Sports like baseball, football, soccer and other out-door activities. Frisbees are also fun to have, just remember, the basic rule of no electricity and no batteries and you should be just fine.

Reading! Books, books and more books! Be sure to gather a good collection of all types of books.

Be sure to include manuals, learning guides, as well as fun fiction for all ages, for the edification and expansion of your mind. These will also make very good barter items someday in the future.

Again, I will remind you that attitude is paramount in all of this and the entire purpose of this book is as a guide to you in forming an effective plan that you will live a victorious and successful life even in tumultuous times.

Without joy there is no victory without victory there is no success so the standard upon which the successful life is measured is that of joy.

In this life we are given choices and these choices are presented to us on a nonstop basis. This begins when you first get out of bed and continues throughout the day to the point of when you're falling asleep in your bed. Thoughts, images and ideas flow through your mind nonstop, all day.

One of the primary points I am trying to share in this work is the need of clarity and the active avoidance of distraction that your thought process might be clear.

Having healthy distraction and fun during times of duress are vital for your heart and soul.

It is your responsibility to take control of your situation, it is your responsibility to decide what you will allow into your mind and when.

Now is the time that you take this control, now is the time that you say no to the media controllers.

Joy and peace are prevented and stolen from the minds of the public to increase the stress levels for the reasons I have mentioned before.

The results of this manipulation are the prevention of peace and joy. This book can stand as a guide to point the reader in the direction away from the manipulation and distraction to a life of fulfillment through the attainment of personal satisfaction found through the enjoyment of the simple things that surround us daily.

This attitude of being positive and the proactive stance of saying no to fear can only be attained by you and you alone. The choices we are given on a moment to moment basis and the information we accept and allow into our minds sets the tone of your day setting the outcome.

The power of your mind is intense and thoughts that you allow to permeate within your mind is the beginning of the manifestation process. I say many times "as above so below" and the truth of this, is that thoughts brought into existence and pondered upon within the mind, sometimes very quickly, are made manifest within our world. The ancients spoke of this, the great teachers have taught this and this is a skill which begins at the core of your existence that must be mastered.

By saying no to fear and by not allowing doubt, worrying and fretting to overtake your thought process you then allow for the positive visualization of success, safety, victory and joy. And that is the goal.

No matter what life has brought to you, no matter what situation you may find yourself in as you read this book, if you allow yourself, you can lift yourself to a higher level, you can rise from the ashes of the past spreading your wings to soar high in the clean clear skies of victory and joy. No matter what the situation.

In closing I will leave you with one great and simple truth and that great truth is that you can do whatever you set your mind to....and that is the sum of all faith and quantum physics in one simple statement.

Now is the time to say no to fear, now is the time to take action now is the time....to rise above.

Epilogue

Upcoming editions in the series will include all of the topics we have covered here but in greater detail. I will expand upon practical application with the addition of tips and tricks and I'm sure you'll find useful. Being a live and fluid situation we are very aware that things can change quickly in this world.

It is because of this very fact it is so important that we have a plan of action that we may be better protected during time of need. Some would say preparation is paranoia, but I say preparation is common sense and common sense in this day and age is less than common. In an ever changing world where we have forces both good and bad vying for position at the top it behooves us as responsible human beings be aware of our surroundings and all times.

The purpose of all these guides is to better aid the reader in the planning process. The basic core of our being and who we are, it is said is formed in childhood and many of the traits of our behavior that we exhibit as adults are the same traits we exhibited as a child.

Children always ask the obvious, children ask the question why? That is the purpose of this first addition is to answer the question of "why". Why society has changed so much, why people are so distracted, why there is such a potential for violence and societal breakdown and above all, why we should prepare.

This book is a standalone work in its own right. The decisions you make are yours and yours alone and this book gives the basics in forming those decisions. If the situation should dictate where the writing of additional books becomes impractical or impossible because of changing geopolitical and economic situations then so be it.

But until that time we will continue on with the series. I hope that you've enjoyed this work and I hope it has been a help.

Until my next book, be well

And....Rise above!

Phoenix Rising.

I will close this volume with one of my favorite quotes from the military science fiction novel "Starship Troopers" published by Robert Heinlein.

A human being should be able to

change a diaper, plan an invasion,

butcher a hog, conn a ship,

design a building, write a sonnet,

balance accounts, build a wall,

set a bone, comfort the dying,

take orders, give orders,

cooperate, act alone,

solve equations, analyze a new problem,

pitch manure, program a computer,

cook a tasty meal, fight efficiently,

and

die gallantly.

Specialization....is for insects.

Words of Wisdom

Fear is only as deep as the mind allows.

Thomas Jefferson

Be not discouraged, but try, ever keep trying; twenty failures are not irremediable if followed by as many undaunted struggles upward; is it not so that mountains are climbed? ~Blavatsky

Wish for nothing so much that you forget to make it come true. ~ Unknown

When you throw dirt, you lose ground. ~Texan Proverb

Life is like riding a bicycle - in order to keep your balance, you must keep moving. ~Albert Einstein

The biggest problem in the world could have been solved when it was small. ~ Unknown

The day will happen whether or not you get up. ~John Ciardi

The only way you may correct the bad things in your past is to add better things to your future. ~Shiloh Morrison

Seek freedom and become captive of your desires. Seek discipline and find your liberty.

~Frank Herbert, Dune Chronicles

You've got a lot of choices. If getting out of bed in the morning is a chore and you're not smiling on a regular basis, try another choice. ~Steven D. Woodhull

Be Content with what you have; rejoice in the way things are. When you realize there is nothing lacking, the whole world belongs to you. ~ Lao Tzu

With each morning's awakening try to live through the day in harmony with the Higher Self. "Try" is the battle-cry taught by the Teachers to each pupil. Naught else is expected of you. One who does his best does all that can be asked. There is a moment when even a Buddha ceases to be a sinning mortal and takes his first step toward Buddhahood. ~ Blavatsky

Good for the body is the work of the body, and good for the soul is the work of the soul, and good for either is the work of the other. ~Henry David Thoreau

One can enjoy a wood fire worthily only when he warms his thoughts by it as well as his hands and feet.

~Odell Shepherd

Remember, if you're headed in the wrong direction, God allows U-turns! ~Allison Gappa Bottke

Don't waste your life in doubts and fears: spend yourself on the work before you, well assured that the right performance of this hour's duties will be the best preparation for the hours or ages that follow it.

Ralph Waldo Emerson

No longer forward nor behind

I look in hope and fear;

But grateful take the good I find,

The best of now and here.

John G. Whittier

It is not work that kills men, it is worry. Work is healthy; you can hardly put more on a man than he can bear. But worry is rust upon the blade. It is not movement that destroys the machinery, but friction.

Henry Ward Beecher

Be just, and fear not.

Let all the ends thou aim'st at be thy country's,

Thy God's and truth's.

William Shakespeare

Never let life's hardships disturb you ... no one can avoid problems, not even saints or sages.

Nichiren Daishonen

Ask yourself this question:

"Will this matter a year from now?"

Richard Carlson, writing in Don't Sweat the Small Stuff

Surely there is something in the unruffled calm of nature that overawes our little anxieties and doubts; the sight of the deep-blue sky and the clustering stars above seems to impart a quiet to the mind.

Jonathan Edwards

Do not anticipate trouble, or worry about what may never happen. Keep in the sunlight.

Benjamin Franklin

Imagine every day to be the last of a life surrounded with hopes, cares, anger and fear. The hours that come unexpectedly will be much the more grateful.

Horace

The mind that is anxious about future events is miserable.

Seneca

Present fears are less than horrible imaginings.

William Shakespeare

Let us be of good cheer, remembering that the misfortunes hardest to bear are those that never happen.

James Russel Lowell

How much pain have cost us the evils that have never happened.

Thomas Jefferson

It is the trouble that never comes that causes the loss of sleep.

Chas. Austin Bates

Live in each season as it passes; breathe the air, drink the drink, taste the fruit, and resign yourself to the influences of each.

Henry David Thoreau

We also deem those happy, who from the experience of life, have learned to bear its ills and without descanting on their weight.

Junvenal

Thus each person by his fears gives wings to rumor, and, without any real source of apprehension, men fear what they themselves have imagined.

Lucan

I never think of the future - it comes soon enough.

Albert Einstein

It is idle to dread what you can-not avoid.

Publius Syrus

He either fears his fate too much,

Or his deserts are small,

Who dares not put it to the touch

To gain or lose it all.

Marquis of Montrose

The rose is fairest when 't is budding new,

and hope is brightest when it dawns from fears.

Walter Scott

It was a high counsel that I once heard given to a young person, "Always do what you are afraid to do."

Ralph Waldo Emerson

Take calculated risks.

That is quite different from being rash.

George S. Patton

Storms make oaks take roots.

Proverb

If you do not hope, you will not find what is beyond your hopes.

St. Clement of Alexandra

We are all inventors, each sailing out on a voyage of discovery, guided each by a private chart, of which there is no duplicate. The world is all gates, all opportunities.

Ralph Waldo Emerson

Seek the lofty by reading, hearing and seeing great work at some moment every day.

Thornton Wilder

The only way of finding the limits of the possible is by going beyond them into the impossible.

Arthur C. Clarke

Without inspiration the best powers of the mind remain dormant. There is a fuel in us which needs to be ignited with sparks.

Johann Gottfried Von Herder

And all may do what has by man been done.

Edward Young

We are what we repeatedly do. Excellence, therefore, is not an act but a habit.

Aristotle

Hope is like the sun, which, as we journey toward it, casts the shadow of our burden behind us.

Samuel Smiles

Work spares us from three evils: boredom, vice, and need.

Voltaire

If the wind will not serve,

take to the oars.

Destitutus ventis, remos adhibe

Latin Proverb

Men's best successes come after their disappointments.

Henry Ward Beecher

You cannot plough a field by

turning it over in your mind.

Author Unknown

The best way out is always through.

Robert Frost

Do not wait to strike till the iron is hot; but make it hot by striking.

William B. Sprague

Nothing will ever be attempted if all possible objections must first be overcome.

Samuel Johnson

Fortune favors the brave.

Publius Terence

When the best things are not possible, the best may be made of those that are. - Richard Hooker

He who hesitates is lost.

Proverb

If you want to succeed in the world must make your own opportunities as you go on. The man who waits for some seventh wave to toss him on dry land will find that the seventh wave is a long time a coming. You can commit no greater folly than to sit by the roadside until someone comes along and invites you to ride with him to wealth or influence.

John B. Gough

Great spirits have always en-countered violent opposition from mediocre minds.

Albert Einstein

Believe with all of your heart that you will do what you were made to do.

Orison Swett Marden

Knowing is not enough; we must apply.

Willing is not enough; we must do.

Johann Wolfgang von Goethe

We are still masters of our fate.

We are still captains of our souls.

Nothing great was ever achieved without enthusiasm.

Ralph Waldo Emerson

For hope is but the dream

of those that wake.

Matthew Prior

Constant dripping hollows out a stone.

Lucretius

Nothing contributes so much to tranquilize the mind as a steady purpose--

a point on which the soul may fix its intellectual eye.

Mary Shelley

Made in the USA
San Bernardino, CA
28 August 2013